CW00621226

Practical
Lean Leadership for
Health Care Managers

A Guide to
Sustainable and Effective
Application of Lean Principles

Kjeld H. Aij, MBA
Bas Lohman

VUmc Amstel Academy

CRC Press
Taylor & Francis Group
Boca Raton   London   New York

CRC Press is an imprint of the
Taylor & Francis Group, an **informa** business

A PRODUCTIVITY PRESS BOOK

CRC Press
Taylor & Francis Group
6000 Broken Sound Parkway NW, Suite 300
Boca Raton, FL 33487-2742

Printed on acid-free paper
Version Date: 20151021

International Standard Book Number-13: 978-1-4987-4802-5 (Paperback)

Visit the Taylor & Francis Web site at
http://www.taylorandfrancis.com

and the CRC Press Web site at
http://www.crcpress.com

Contents

Overview of Boxes

Cast of Characters

At Careville UMC:

Omar **Al Assaf**	Laboratory manager at Careville UMC
Cameron **Morton**	Division D director of operations
Jonathan **Foster**	Emergency room (ER) team leader
Jeanne **Smith**	ER department head
Susan **Fernandez**	Division D care manager
Rachel **Jameson**	ER department head at a community hospital
Peter **Jacobs**	Chairman of the Division B board and cardiologist
Jessica **Kern**	HR advisor
Ellen **Kowalski**	Division B care manager
Bob **Patterson**	Member of the board of directors
Robert **Quinn**	Experienced Lean consultant
Frank **Johnson**	Head of the hospital pharmacy
Marjorie **Walker**	New director of operations, Morton's replacement
Linda **Townsend**	Division D staff advisor
Luis **Torres**	Strategy & policy director
Carl **McLaughlin**	Medical head of the ER
Tom **Black**	Jeanne Smith's husband

At the Robert Kennedy Hospital (Oregon):

Agnes **Karlsson**	Lean program manager
Margo **Davidson**	Strategy & policy director
Ingrid **Pearson**	Member of the board of directors
Eric **Taylor**	Head of the ER
Jacob **Vargas**	HR director

Foreword

Before you lies an important book. The application of Lean principles and methods in health care to improve care processes has grown explosively in recent years. However, Lean can only make a sustainable contribution if implementation increases the problem-solving capacities of professionals, teams, and—ultimately—entire care institutions. Leadership is essential to this process.

Lean is sometimes used as little more than a toolkit for analyzing, organizing, and managing processes. If successful, this reduces waste and patients experience more value. If it goes too far, the Lean and mean attitude can result in organizational anorexia. This is common in the business world. Lean is sometimes deployed primarily to improve processes that are part of daily operations in the workplace. If this goes well, problems are identified sooner and the thinking capacities and practical knowledge of workers are used to tackle problems more effectively. If it goes too far, daily and weekly sessions become an end in themselves and motivated professionals lose interest because they no longer consider them relevant. Lean really works well only if these two approaches are implemented in a balanced way and bound by the third element of personal growth through process improvement. This links improvement to a sense of purpose and learning. To me, this is the core challenge for Lean leadership.

This book uses a case story to present the familiar struggles involved in applying seemingly logical theory to daily practice. Lean requires behavioral change and that in turn demands change skills and leadership qualities. By putting daily practice first and using theory to support the learning points it presents, the book respects a key Lean principle: improve based on practical experience—or, in other words, "go to the source." This book is particularly valuable because it is the product of two authors who work with Lean daily in the workplace.

I see the fact that this book is being published at this time as a sign that implementation of Lean in health care has reached the next level. The discussions within the "Lean in health care" (Lidz) network clearly demonstrate that Lean needs are shifting from "what" to "how." After a few years of experiments to determine whether Lean can make a meaningful contribution to health care, we have now reached the stage of figuring out how to make it work, respecting every detail and characteristic quality of health care. The learning points for Lean leadership are not health care specific; therefore, the book is also interesting for the business community because the challenges of working in a Lean way are equally great.

I hope you enjoy the book and draw inspiration for successful Lean leadership in your own daily practice.

Marc Rouppe van der Voort, PhD
Manager, Lean and Logistics at St. Antonius Hospital, Nieuwegein, the Netherlands
Chairman of the Dutch Lean in Health Care Network (Lidz)

Authors

Kjeld Aij is a business administrator and registered nurse with an MBA with more than fifteen years of experience in the health care industry, where he has held a number of managerial positions. He worked as the head of Anesthesiology & Operative Care at VU University Medical Center from 2010 to mid-2015. In April 2015, he became the Director of Business Administration for the Acute Care Division at VU University Medical Center. In the past three years, Kjeld has implemented various projects in the areas of quality and patient safety and spearheaded, among other projects, the introduction of Lean thinking and Lean processes in the operating theaters.

Kjeld earned an MBA from Business School Nederland and has previously conducted research into leadership and successful change in organizations, with a special focus on the role of middle management. Since 2010, he has served as a member of the project committee for the Dutch Operating Room Benchmarking Collaborative, whose objective is to improve operating theater performance through mutual learning from best practices. In 2010, Kjeld was appointed a research member of the Lean Healthcare Research Consortium of Stanford University in Palo Alto, California. Since 2013, he has been a member of the Center for Lean Healthcare Research of Ohio State University's Fisher College of Business.

He has recently finished his PhD thesis at VU University of Amsterdam, investigating the leadership behaviors essential to the successful, sustainable implementation of Lean principles in hospitals. In 2014, Kjeld became a member of the Human Capital Research Consortium of the Faculty of Economics and Business Administration at VU University, Amsterdam.

Kjeld organizes a number of workshops and seminars each year and is often asked to speak at conferences. He is also an entrepreneur and was co-owner of an IT company in health care, where he applied Lean principles.

Bas Lohman studied economics at the VU University Amsterdam and is operational manager of Gynecology and Pediatrics at the Albert Schweitzer Hospital in Dordrecht, the Netherlands. Earlier in his career he was a Lean coach at the VU University Medical Center. Part of his job was to support line management in using Lean principles. Before that, he supported similar processes in a variety of sectors as a consultant, with a particular interest in banking and insurance. He feels the social involvement and relevance of health care are key motivators for continuously seeking out possibilities for improvement.

Bas previously published the book *Practical Lean Management* (2010, Maj Engineering Publishing), coauthored with Van Os. This book describes various Lean tools based on the stages an organization may go through during Lean implementation. The book also addresses change management to ensure successful Lean implementation. *Practical Lean Leadership for Health Care Managers* is not a sequel, but is an excellent companion to *Practical Lean Management*. Bas regularly gives lectures and workshops in addition to his day job.

Contributors

Peter Fest is an independent project and program manager, coach, and consultant in performance support. He has held a variety of managerial positions in profit and nonprofit organizations, all focused on the interface between performance and development. Over the past decade, his work in the health care sector has inspired him. He is motivated by a desire to unite the passion professionals have for their patients and clients with the growing need for more commercial attitudes and action.

Peter considers Lean to be an important principle for connecting quality improvement and process optimization. He is always looking for factors that define successful leadership. He considers this book to be a milestone and is looking forward to taking you, the reader, on the journey toward sustainable, effective Lean leadership.

Michiel van Geloven took the lead on the case story that runs through the book, while Peter focused on the in-depth boxes.

Michiel van Geloven is an independent project manager and consultant. He has more than twenty years of experience in both consulting and managerial positions. He is often involved with innovation projects in higher education as a project manager or consultant. Key themes in his work include the application of information technology, sustainability of project results, and the quality of cooperation. He is often asked to perform external reviews of internal projects by organizations within his extensive network.

Michiel is a prolific writer and has the ability to quickly make himself at home in a new field. He regularly contributes to publications on a broad range of subjects, from business cases for digital testing to health care administration. The intriguing and rich world of Lean and leadership adds another topic to this spectrum.

For more information, visit: www.interimichiel.nl.

Acknowledgments

The Careville UMC case study is the common thread in this book. The case study provides the reader with insights into the development of leadership in relation to the introduction of Lean. The setting and hospital name are fictitious and any resemblance to persons or organizations is purely coincidental.

The authors presented *Practical Lean Leadership for Health Care Managers* to a number of Lean experts and people with Lean experience to ensure the book is consistent with the realities of health care. We are eternally grateful to the following individuals for their constructive criticism and incisive insights: Tessa Biesheuvel, Joost van Galen, Ingrid Gerstel, Emile Lohman, Marco van der Noordaa, and Marc Rouppe van der Voort.

VU University Medical Center Amstel Academy/VU University Medical Center Academy represents innovative education and excellent education and training. This book was realized in part on the initiative of the VU University Medical Center Amstel Academy. With this and other books and in cooperation with regional and national health care institutions, the VU University Medical Center Amstel Academy contributes to patient safety and quality of care.

Introduction

This book focuses on the importance of leadership in the implementation of Lean in health care. As a management philosophy, Lean is making strong headway in health care and experience has shown that leadership is an essential but not self-evident element. Lean is a management philosophy for achieving sustainable improvement and reducing waste in processes. The application of Lean tools appears relatively simple, but the change in management culture required to turn Lean into a lasting success requires strong leadership. Previously published books of case stories about Lean in health care illustrate the successes, lessons learned, and challenges for the future. This book continues where other books on Lean left off, but is also different because it describes a search for the essence of and success factors for *Lean in relation to leadership*.

We will take you on a journey to discover the secrets of a successful Lean leader. *Practical Lean Leadership for Health Care Managers* is primarily written for managers in health care, focusing specifically on department heads with some Lean experience. We have also written this book based on our own experiences in health care and assume that many of the principles will also apply in other sectors, both public and private.

We describe our search for the secret of Lean leadership based on a case study told as a story, in which we follow the introduction and development of Lean in a large hospital. We support the case study with theory presented in boxes. The structure of this book is explained later in this Introduction, but first, we invite you into the time machine. Does this sound familiar?

The Past

A Saturday, the second weekend of spring break. Downtown is still deserted, everyone is at the beach. The emergency room (ER) at the Careville UMC is operating on a skeleton crew. After a quiet handoff, the evening shift team sits around talking about the beautiful spring day. The blush of springtime is still in the air; people are shopping, doing a bit of gardening, taking a swim in the sea, or just relaxing.

At around 6:30 PM, it is as if a bomb exploded somewhere: six deathly ill elderly patients, three casualties from car accidents, two men who had gotten into a fight, all kinds of people with a variety of athletic injuries, and one individual with massive blood loss following an encounter with an electric hedge trimmer. All within fifteen minutes. A quarter of an hour later, the department head and team leader arrive, summoned by a panicked phone call from an ER nurse. They walk straight into a chaos of disorganized nurses, irritable doctors, complaining patients, angry family members, and a security guard who is trying to keep the two fighters away from each other.

Straight to work. The department head quickly assesses the severity of the situation and calls home to say she's going to be a while—even though she's not even on call. She also begs her team leader to stay and get into the thick of it. Within the hour, her shirt has more sweat stains than dry patches. She simply cannot calm the patients and their families.

She's also in conflict with ER doctors who cannot help out. On top of it all, she also had to take care of a crying young nurse who is at the end of her rope.

Some of the equipment is not where it's supposed to be or is not working properly. The hospital dispatch is having no luck getting ahold of the on-call technician.

Patient flows are not as they should be; the same patient is repeatedly seen first by a physician assistant and then by two different doctors, who move straight on to the next patient without finishing their work. There is also a long line at the front desk because the least stress-resistant receptionist happens to be working today. Even the perpetually cool-headed team leader is having trouble managing the situation and is running around putting out brushfires.

It's midnight before order has been restored and the department head and team leader feel comfortable going home. Fortunately, there were no medical incidents and no major errors of judgment appear to have been made. But the department head is sure that at least one patient is going to file an official complaint. She is already dreading the time-consuming procedure.

Later

A Saturday, the second weekend of spring break. Downtown is still deserted, everyone is at the beach. But the ER at the Careville UMC is fully staffed. This decision was taken based on a statistical analysis of historical data. Due to the expected pressure in months to come, management also decided to explicitly draw the attention of ER nurses and doctors to the triage protocol. Having a number of colleagues on standby is standard practice.

At around 6:30 PM, it is as if a bomb exploded somewhere: six deathly ill elderly patients, three casualties from car accidents, two men who had gotten into a fight, all kinds of people with a variety of athletic injuries, and one individual with massive blood loss following an encounter with an electric hedge trimmer. All within fifteen minutes. The two fighters are separated immediately.

As expected, triage is performed without a hitch. Everybody knows their task. Work is swift and orderly. The coordinating nurse calls the team leader, who has a day off, and briefly describes the situation. The team leader decides to call in the consultant, as well as the standby consultant. He promises to call the Medicine and Surgical residents himself and ask them to stay on standby. Clear agreements have been made about this. They are also aware that today is potentially a peak day and are prepared for the workload.

The team leader knows that each piece of equipment not only has its own place but also that there are enough spares available, which are tested weekly. He does not need to call his department head. That only becomes necessary if the coordinating nurse calls back an hour later and reports that the situation is no longer sufficiently under control. In forty-five minutes, the nurse will call a time-out in consultation with the ER doctor and "weigh" the seriousness of the situation.

Before the team leader goes back to enjoying his time off, his thoughts wander to the current situation in the ER. He smiles contentedly at the thought that every patient will only be seen by one doctor after triage. The doctor will have immediate access to the up-to-date medical chart on his iPad, so he needs to ask the patient only a few additional questions. He has called the Medicine and Surgical residents and he is counting on the fact that they will provide support of their own accord.

Around 8 PM, he glances down at his watch and realizes that the situation in the ER has returned to normal. After all, they didn't call. A potential evening of chaos has been nipped in the bud—it is just another day at the office.

Still—as scheduled in advance—they will do an in-depth evaluation on Monday. Minor mistakes will have been made and it is always important to learn from them. The additional workload will be a topic for discussion in his next report to the operations manager. The latter will doubtless have insightful questions to stimulate further improvement. The next "target situation" is for the department to have the capacity to address peak moments entirely independently. This will allow the team leader to enjoy his weekend off without disruption.

Lean in Health Care

This book focuses on leadership in health care practice. We devote only limited attention to the general theory underlying Lean.

Reading Guide

In this book, we will introduce you to Jeanne Smith, ER Department head of the fictional Careville UMC and her (international) colleagues. You follow her in the quest for the secrets to Lean in health care, focused on the role of the leader. You will witness her development and what happens to her superiors and the managers around her.

The story (case study) is regularly interrupted by a box in which we elaborate (the theory behind) a certain aspect or theme. You can skip these boxes and return to them at a later time. However, they often contribute to a better understanding of the storyline. The boxes can also be read on their own.

We recommend reading the case study—and thus the chapters—in chronological order. This will let you experience how Smith and the other protagonists explore and grown.

The first chapters begin with a presentation of a few key points based on questions. This is a warm-up exercise that you may skip if you wish. Starting from Chapter 3, we will jump right into the rest of the story.

We conclude with a brief introduction of each chapter:

- In Chapter 1, the idea to use Lean is born.
- In Chapter 2, a Lean pilot is launched in the ER.
- In Chapter 3, a tale of two pilots: "it was the best of times, it was the worst of times" is presented.
- In Chapter 4, Lean spreads past the ER.
- In Chapter 5, an international internship with the protagonist is described.
- In Chapter 6, Lean affects the entire organization: a program is being prepared.
- In Chapter 7, a Lean program is implemented.

- In Chapter 8, a situation at Careville UMC in a few years is presented.
- The Epilogue is a brief look back on this book.

Each chapter ends with reflection on the key learning points presented in the chapter. We use these to gather the properties we consider important in a Lean leader. We present these as pieces of a puzzle. Our aim is to complete the puzzle of properties a Lean leader must possess.

1

Lean in the Picture

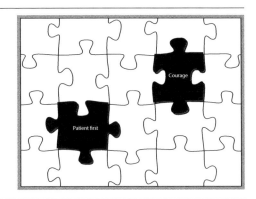

Before We Get Started

Lean Comes from the Automobile Industry—Patients Are Not Cars!

Lean was born in the automobile industry; Toyota is the founder of Lean and still considered a global benchmark. However, "Lean" was not coined by Toyota, but by John Krafcik, a student at MIT. He was doing research for Jim Womack, founder of the Lean Enterprise Institute, who ultimately wrote a book together with Jones and Roos entitled *The Machine That Changed the World* (1991). A number of industries have since adopted the Lean mentality, among other reasons, because processes and information streams are commonplace. Lean has taken root in the financial sector and is currently being adopted in many others, including health care.

How Can You Get Started with Lean and How Fast Does It Yield Results?

The introduction of Lean within a care institution usually starts with a pilot project in one department. A Lean consultant is often hired to get things off to a running start, to support the process, and to train employees. This allows short-term gains, such as less waste of time and money and fewer errors. Achieving sustainable effects requires stamina; a limited pilot project is not enough and does not reflect the potential power and scope of Lean. Increasing problem-solving capacities is also necessary.

Can the Implementation of Lean Be Considered a Project?

Lean implementation usually begins as a project. However, a project is by its very definition finite, while Lean represents a permanent approach, a philosophy. Organization-wide implementation of Lean is more like a transition or transformation, but a project-based approach can be a good first step. After getting started with a pilot project, a program designed to shape the Lean transformation is often the next step. The introduction of Lean is impossible without leadership, particularly in the longer term.

Our Organization Does Not Use Lean at All. Can I Introduce It Solely within My Own Department?

It is perfectly viable to start with a single department. However, you will notice that there are interactions and interferences with other departments that you cannot get around. To really experience the benefits of Lean, cooperation with other departments is required. This means that it is essential to create broad support from the very start.

Case Study

In this book, we take you on a journey to Careville UMC, an academic hospital that provides high-quality specialist medical care, but is not a pioneer where modern management is concerned. Careville UMC has about 820 beds, over 6,150 employees, and handles over 64,000 admissions per year. In this case study, you follow one of the department heads, who has decided to introduce Lean in her own department: the emergency room (ER). Watch as her thinking develops, how she tries to convince colleagues to participate, and in doing so, discovers the key factor for turning Lean into a success. She quickly and repeatedly discovers that the road to success is not without challenges. The case study continues in the following chapters. The chapters should be read in order.

This chapter presents the following people:

Cameron **Morton.** Operational director for Division D (which includes the ER). A born administrator and not particularly creative. Has been working for Careville UMC since it was founded. Holds a degree in business economics. When it comes to claiming credit for success, he is always first in line.

Jonathan **Foster.** Third-generation Jamaican, studied physical therapy in Canada, interned in Johannesburg, and then spent 5 years in the Asklepios Hospital, where he was introduced to Lean.

Jeanne **Smith.** ER department head and protagonist of this book. On the career fast track, she made ER department head before the age of 30. She is an avid reader and enjoys water sports in her spare time.

Susan **Fernandez.** Care manager for Division D. A skilled but careful manager who does not like to take chances.

Rachel **Jameson.** ER department head in a private hospital, who has been actively using Lean for a year. Went to college with Smith.

Jessica **Kern.** Human resources (HR) advisor. An elderly lady who lives alone with her three cats and grows begonias in the greenhouse in her backyard. Also plays a mean game of squash.

Bob **Patterson.** General practitioner by training, joined the Board of Directors 3 years ago. Divorced last year and drives a Cadillac.

Robert **Quinn.** An experienced Lean consultant who has been working for a midsize consultancy for a few years. Is learning Japanese because he dreams of taking a long trip to the Mecca of Lean.

Linda **Townsend.** Staff consultant for Division D, an enthusiastic young go-getter eager to learn new things.

Luis **Torres.** Strategy and policy director. An old hand, has been working at Careville UMC for 15 years. Is passionate about the place and the people who work there.

Carl **McLaughlin.** Medical head of the ER. A reliable, hardworking, and honest doctor. He has three teenage kids and an artistic wife who sometimes keep him up at night.

Tom **Black.** Jeanne Smith's husband. Teaches advanced placement economics at a local high school.

Motivation

Jeanne Smith, ER department head at Careville UMC, recently attended a national congress on Lean in health care. She believes that her department could perform much better than it does, but cannot put her finger on what the problem is. She regularly has to deal with angry or crying coworkers faced with mistakes, processes that grind to a halt, frustrated patients, and so on, while cost-cutting continues unabated. She had heard of Lean before and it had piqued her interest, but she has not done anything with it yet.

Discovering Lean

The conference is an eye opener. Speakers with real-world experience show how they took care quality to the next level with Lean thinking and methods. Almost in passing, Smith discovers significant savings are frequently also possible, but that seems to be of secondary interest to most speakers. "I want that, too," she thinks to herself. Back home, she immediately starts looking for more information, and the next morning at the hospital she tries to find out whether somebody at Careville UMC is already using Lean. That does not appear to be the case. In fact, most people she talks to know nothing more than the name.

She spends the weekend delving into the books about Lean she ordered, one of which is about health care: *Lean Thinking and Action in Health Care* (Benders, Rouppe van der Voort, and Berden, 2010). On Sunday afternoon, her mind is made up: she is going to introduce Lean in the ER! The next morning, she has her bi-monthly meeting with her director of operations, Cameron Morton. She enthusiastically presents her plan, to a tepid response: "If you think it's worth a shot, go ahead. Just make sure the ER keeps running!"

Smith is not easily discouraged, though she cannot find the time to make plans during the rest of the day. After the last meeting, she processes a pile of e-mails and runs to catch the train. Back home, she chats with her husband Tom while he cooks. After dinner, Smith dives back into her Lean books, trying to figure out where to start. When they sit down for a glass of wine together, she concludes that she will need a lot more information. "What do you know about Lean?" she asks her husband. "Toyota," he immediately responds. But he does not get much further than that, although Smith's enthusiasm is infectious. They talk until the bottle is empty and the hour late, both enchanted by Lean.

It is a busy week and the evening talks at home are the extent of Lean development. Smith has her hands full getting her regular work done and has no time to make plans. On Friday night, too tired to sleep, she frets about ways to find the time to realize her ambitious plans. The next morning, when her husband comes home with the weekly groceries, he also brings another book about Lean in health care. She dives right in and they spend the evening dissecting it. They conclude that there are a great many challenges facing the implementation of Lean in the workplace and leadership is certainly one of them. How do you set a course, create broad support and ensure actual results? "Covey," says Tom, "are you familiar with his eighth characteristic of effective leadership? Something like: 'Find your voice and inspire others to find theirs.' Oh, and also 'Begin with the end in mind.' You'll need that, too."

At a party on Sunday afternoon, Smith is drawn into a conversation with someone who works for a major bank, where they started introducing Lean last year. Obviously, a bank is not a hospital, but she still sees a lot of parallels where smarter process design and removing waste are concerned. Her enthusiasm continues to grow. Back at the hospital, she immediately makes an appointment with Luis Torres, director of strategy and policy. She also sends a few messages to old college friends—with success: the same week, she has a pleasant, long phone conversation with Rachel Jameson, who like her, is head of an ER and has been working with Lean for over a year. She learns working with Lean is not easy and that she will definitely need a Lean consultant—which means she needs a budget, which is going to be a challenge. Then she is off to meeting after meeting … Jameson also points her to Manfred Kets de Vries: "He's an interesting Dutch leadership expert. I particularly like how he draws attention to the irrational components of people's behavior, especially at work, and the risks this entails. That insight helped us explain and address the resistance we met introducing of Lean at our hospital."

The next day kicks off with a meeting with the departmental HR advisor, Jessica Kern. Smith asked permission to hire a new team leader to replace someone who retired a while back and she is finally getting the green light. They discuss the text for the job opening and other details and Kern promises to put the ad online this week. Later that day, Smith realizes that this is an opportunity to hire someone with a Lean background—she immediately calls Kern and asks her to add one more line to the job description. Although Kern has no clue what Lean is, she agrees to the change after some prompting. Smith tackles another pile of paperwork, processes a few changes and is off to catch her train with a spring in her step. It is raining, but that cannot ruin her mood. Slowly but surely, she sees her plans taking shape.

Initial Resistance

During her next meeting with the division's care manager, Susan Fernandez, she enthusiastically talks about Lean and everything she has read about. "Wonderful," she says, "but what's it going to cost?" Smith replies that she is far more interested in the potential gains—and everything shows those are significant! Fernandez is not easily convinced and asks her how it will affect care in the ER. "We can't afford to take any risks there, Jeanne," she says. "Lean is all about improving quality," says Smith. "Yes, I know that," replies Fernandez, "but what about the costs?" Hesitantly, Smith confesses that yes, as is often the case, an upfront investment will be required. However, she expects the additional costs to be modest: if they use the available education budget to train the department, they do not need to figure out a way to cover the costs of a Lean consultant. Fernandez refers her to Morton to talk funding, lamenting the fact that there really is no money, and ends the meeting. Smith is fuming, but the rest of her day is filled with other issues to contend with. Only when she gets home does she realize just how angry she is. Her husband takes her out to clear her head and they discuss Fernandez's attitude while they walk. "Too bad she won't support you more," says Tom.

Fortunately, her meeting with the Director of Strategy and Policy is more productive. Torres takes her very seriously. He has read about Lean, but never saw the opportunity to put it on the Careville UMC agenda. He immediately agrees to look for budget for a Lean consultant and will also inform Patterson, who is on the Board of Directors. He is confident that Patterson will be interested in supporting an experiment like this. "Patterson is a big fan of Bennis" says Torres. "He's always saying 'The manager accepts the status quo; the leader challenges it,' to anyone who will listen. I'm guessing he'll admire your chutzpah."

Encouraged, Smith gets back to work with a grin on her face. When she arrives, she finds a callback request from Kern: there are 44 applicants for the team leader position. Later that day, the pile of letters and resumes lands on her desk, and she stuffs them in her bag to browse through at home. Toward the end of the afternoon, Smith has a meeting with Carl McLaughlin, medical head of the ER. She briefly describes the conference she attended. McLaughlin says that he is willing to support the experiment with Lean because he agrees there is a lot of room for improvement in the ER.

While her husband grades tests, Smith goes through the pile of letters and resumes. She discards over half immediately as unfit for the job. One letter in particular catches her eye: someone who has been working with Lean for 3 years in his current position. His other experience and training also looks promising, so she puts him at the top of her list. Later that week, after discussing the applicants with the selection committee, three other candidates remain in addition to this man. Kern immediately schedules the interviews to expedite the procedure. In the meanwhile, Smith does a little more reading about Lean to figure out which questions she needs to ask to discover what "her" candidate really knows about Lean, and how valuable that knowledge is. She discusses it with her colleague Jameson and forms an idea of how to approach it.

Shortly before the job interviews, Smith calls Torres about the status of her budget request. Unfortunately, he is not at work and his secretary does not know the details. During the job interviews, she notices that she has already written off the first three candidates—the "Lean man" is last in line. Biased as she is, she immediately thinks he is the best man for the job. She has to do her best not to push too hard during the evaluation with the interview committee and has to bite her tongue not to reject the other three candidates—who certainly gave a good interview—out of hand. Fortunately, the committee finally sees things her way and agrees that her favorite—Jonathan Foster—is the right candidate.

The Lean Adventure Can Begin

That week gets even better, because she runs into Torres on Friday afternoon, who informs her that he is all but done creating an initial budget for a Lean consultant. Since Smith has a lot to get done that afternoon, she asks Linda Townsend, one of the division staff consultants, to start looking into organizations they can approach for a Lean consultant. Townsend is immediately enthusiastic and Smith realizes that she should have involved her sooner. It is well past 6 PM when Smith decides to call it a day. But she runs into Townsend in the hallway, who has discovered some interesting things. They decide to discuss Lean over a drink. Townsend is completely on board with the idea and will ask her line manager if she can free up time for the project. She has more than enough on her plate with management contract, care pathways, and a fairly complex project involving the introduction of a new sandwich cart. Smith loves the fact that Townsend has already started reading about Lean. She somewhat hesitantly admits that she is enthusiastic about Kotter's eight-step process for implementing change. When she notices Smith is also doing her research, she goes a step further: "How will we create a guiding coalition, Jeanne?" An interesting discussion ensues and they determine that Torres and Patterson are a solid link to the top of the organization.

On Tuesday, she continues her discussion about potential Lean consultants with Townsend. When she walks into Torres' office afterward, he cheerfully announces that she can get started: she has her budget. He will confirm it formally and also discuss it with Morton to make sure that he does not throw up any roadblocks, he says with a grin. He knows his customers. "There's only one 'but'," he says. Smith knows how these things go, so she is not worried. "We will use your initiative as a pilot, but also as leverage to get Lean onto the policy agenda. "So I can do my thing and the whole hospital will be watching," says Smith. "Pretty much," says Torres, assuring her she has his full support. Back in her office, she gets a call from Kern, informing her that her "Lean man" has said yes, and the best news is that he can start in 6 weeks. Her last meeting of the day is with Fernandez, who proposes she get the "Lean" project off to a running start and immediately offers to supervise the project. This sounds great and Smith goes home in high spirits.

While she cooks, she tells her husband about her day. A little worried, he wonders if having Fernandez as the sponsor is a wise choice. "After all," he says, "she doesn't own the problem and is currently not particularly invested in the project's success. Wouldn't Luis Torres be a better sponsor for you?" he asks. "That's actually a really good point. After all, he's actively involved and a stakeholder. Susan will need to be part of the steering committee though," says Smith. They continue to talk, discussing how to play this out without offending Fernandez.

The next morning at the hospital, Smith and Townsend talk to a number of consultancy firms. Both are particularly impressed with one agency and decide to ask them to draw up an offer. They have already gauged what it will cost them and it looks like they will stay within budget. Townsend has started working on the project proposal and is pestering Smith with all kinds of questions. Defining the problem appears to be the biggest challenge because, while Smith can easily identify 10 bottlenecks in the ER, she cannot quite put her finger on the most urgent reason to start using Lean. So she calls Jameson again. "Oh," she says, "I'm sure you have disappointing patient satisfaction figures or wait times that are longer than you would like. Those are great places to start." "Thanks, that's a good starting point, I should have thought of that on my own!" says Smith. Those are issues a lot of employees complain to her about. She sends Townsend an e-mail, asking her to dig up the relevant figures, and runs off to her next meeting (Box 1.1).

BOX 1.1   DEFINING LEAN TERMINOLOGY

This list provides an overview of a number of Lean concepts that are important in this book. We refer you to the Lean literature for more detailed explanations and terminology.

- 5S Methodology for organizing the workplace to support procedures and keep it neat and tidy. The goal is to eliminate waste due to searching, disorder, and contamination. 5S stands for sorting, streamlining, systematic cleaning, standardizing, and sustaining.
- 5 Whys: Typical "Lean method" for identifying the cause of a problem. By continuing to ask "why" in response to the answers you receive, you will

(Continued)

BOX 1.1 (*CONTINUED*)   DEFINING LEAN TERMINOLOGY

discover the root cause of a problem is often very different from what it may seem. Note: Ask why, not who! If the analysis reveals the cause is a single person, the analysis was most likely not performed correctly.

- Flow: Unimpeded, uninterrupted flow of the product or service through the process toward the patient. Or the unimpeded, uninterrupted progress of the patient through the care process.
- Gemba: Japanese for "workplace," the place where direct value is added for the patient. This could be the operating room, ER, nursing ward, and so on.
- Kaizen: Japanese for continuous improvement. Companies strive for improvement by identifying, analyzing, and solving problems both large and small in a structural way, and planning, implementing, and safeguarding the solution. Everything is designed to serve an ultimate destination, the organization's "true north."
- KPI: Key performance indicators are the desired measurable characteristics of the process that must ensure that the result meets patient or client demands.
- Spaghetti chart: Method for identifying waste due to unnecessary employee movements. The diagram is a scale drawing of a workplace, including all points an employee must go to complete his task. All employee movements are drawn in based on observation. The fuller the "plate" of spaghetti, the more likely there is some unnecessary movement.
- Standard procedure: The best way to perform a procedure at any given moment, determined by the team and management. Managers must also ensure that work is only done according to this procedure. This goes beyond creating a protocol, but requires continuous attention and discipline. If the standard procedure is not followed, this indicates instability in the process.
- Stand-up meeting: Moments when a team comes together and reports on the events of the day to their manager. Employees actually stand during the stand-up meeting—this has been proven to contribute to a more active attitude. A stand-up meeting generally lasts no longer than 15 minutes and takes place daily. The goal is to provide the leader and employees with a forum where problems can be identified and addressed immediately.
- True north: The ultimate destination an organization works toward. However, a true north is so far away that it will likely never be reached, but a great deal can be gained by traveling the road toward it. Example of Toyota's true north: build a car that can drive from coast to coast on a single tank of gas and clean the air.
- Visual management: The principle that performance in the areas of care delivered must be visible to everyone involved to make deviations immediately visible and actionable. Signals must be simple and visible at a glance. People need to know what they have to do when a deviation becomes visible.

(Continued)

BOX 1.1 (*CONTINUED*)   DEFINING LEAN TERMINOLOGY

- Value: The provided specifications, the right moment, and the right price at which products or services can be supplied for the patient or customer.

- Value stream mapping: This type of analysis is required when you want to design a process that provides maximum value for the patient: no waiting, errors, or other waste, getting it right the first time. This requires a clear picture of the current state. A value stream map charts all process steps completed by a patient, including side effects, actions, processing time, wait time, and information streams that contribute to the end result. For example: In the ER, a medical chart is created for each new patient, consisting of a binder with a set of forms and tabs. Some receptionists work diligently to make sure that there is a large stack of binders with empty forms. However, if the forms change, all of the folders need to be rearranged. Advance work in this case is double work. A value stream map will identify this.

The offer from the Lean consultant soon arrives and Smith presents it to Torres. He frowns at the total amount. "I wasn't counting on this," he says. "Well," says Smith, "it does extend into next year. Is there something we can do with that, like shift some to the new budget?" Torres will have to take another look and suggests they arrange an introductory meeting with the proposed consultant. Smith is ready to go. But before she does, she asks Torres if he is willing to assume the role of sponsor. "Of course, Jeanne! I would love to, and it seems like the logical choice. Who will be in the steering committee?" They come to the conclusion that the steering committee should consist of Torres, who will be the chairman; Fernandez; Morton on behalf of division management; and Smith as a user representative. They consider asking McLaughlin, but decide against it for now, considering his already very busy schedule.

Within a week, Smith, Townsend, and one other colleague have a meeting with Robert Quinn, a calm and trustworthy 30-something-year-old. Smith grills him thoroughly, but he has an answer to every question. And when they discover he's available soon, the choice practically makes itself. They decide to hire him and agree that he will initially be helping fine-tune the project plan to allow a strong start.

The Project Plan

Quinn starts working at Careville UMC at the same time as Smith's new team leader, Foster. Smith decides to put both on the project. Townsend is also included and she feels that her dream team is complete. "Robert, Linda, could you get started on writing the project plan?" asks Smith. They gladly accept, and agree to meet again in a week. Smith asks Foster if he has time for lunch, so they can get to know each other a little better. Lunchtime discussion quickly veers toward Lean, of course. Smith asks Foster a barrage of questions and the conversation soon moves to the Lean roles he experienced at the Asklepios Hospital. He sketches a fairly solid outline, but unfortunately there is no time to examine the matter in depth. "Let's have lunch together again soon, Jonathan," says Smith in parting, "I want to know everything!" (Box 1.2).

BOX 1.2 A "STANDARDIZED" APPROACH TO IMPLEMENTING LEAN?

When an organization decides to start using Lean, the question of how to approach it quickly arises. There is no one-size-fits-all approach—each organization has its unique operations and culture, so the focus of a Lean implementation will differ. In this box, we outline a possible approach that includes many of the basic components of a Lean approach.

A program-based approach is recommended for organization-wide Lean implementation. In this case study, startup is limited to one department, the ER, which the Board of Directors considers a pilot project for subsequent large-scale implementation. A project-based approach to such a pilot is strongly recommended.

A project requires a steering committee, a group that steers the course of the project in broad strokes. The steering committee has the final responsibility and decides on progress. Members of the steering committee are responsible for coordinating with their constituents. This role is particularly important in this case, considering the potential for future expansion of Lean to the rest of the organization.

This steering committee should be kept compact to allow efficient decision making. The roles of chairman/sponsor, senior supplier, and senior user must be represented as a minimum requirement (Van Geloven, Fest, and De Roos, 2012).

Smith is wise to carefully consider steering committee membership. Having the right representatives in each role can have a strong positive influence on the project and thus the future introduction of Lean. A wrong choice can lead to

- A project following a suboptimal course (three steps forward, two steps back)
- A steering committee founded under internal pressure
- A steering committee that needs to be kept in line and supported by the project leader, rather than the reverse

Given these considerations, Smith is making the right decision choosing Torres over Fernandez as sponsor. This is also in the best interest of future expansion. From a Lean perspective, Fernandez would be the most suitable sponsor; she is a line management representative and not, like Torres, a staff manager.

This approach is consistent with the one chosen by Careville UMC. Two key pillars of a Lean approach are the introduction of operational management and learning to improve using Lean tools. Four main process stages can be distinguished, which in practice will partially run parallel to each other or may overlap.

INITIATION PHASE

During the initiation phase, all issues related to correct organization of the program are examined. The foundations for the program are laid and the plan is elaborated. Relevant questions include:

- How can the program goals be lined up with those of the organization?
- How will the program help realize these goals?

(Continued)

BOX 1.2 (*CONTINUED*)   A "STANDARDIZED" APPROACH TO IMPLEMENTING LEAN?

- How do other active projects and programs relate to the Lean program?
- How do we create a plan and program management?
- Which departments and processes will be addressed first?

During this phase, both top-down and bottom-up approaches to Lean initiatives are possible. Without commitment from the Board, however, local initiatives risk bleeding out. This is because care chain dependencies are often essential for addressing cross-departmental problems. "Silo thinking" can lead to processes being organized so that they are optimal for department A, but suboptimal for department B. Active and facilitating leadership across departments is crucial to ensure focus and ambition is aimed at the coherent whole.

Careville UMC is choosing to run a pilot project in the ER first. Under many circumstances, this is a good way to collect evidence, fine-tune the approach and strengthen support from the Board. The principles and phases described here also apply to a pilot project.

ANALYSIS PHASE

During this phase, the organization and current processes are analyzed by interviewing employees, managers, and if appropriate, clients. But also by using tools from the "Lean toolbox," such as a value stream map, gemba walks, and spaghetti charts. This creates a picture of the current situation within the selected processes. See Box 1.1 for an explanation of this and other Lean terminology.

You will also look at how operational management is organized. The ability to perform good and swift course adjustments is essential, not only to process control but also for continuous improvement. The reporting structure often needs to be changed to realize this.

REDESIGN PHASE

During this phase, often the most intensive, two processes run parallel: process optimization and reorganization of the reporting structure. Workshops help chart the "future state" of the processes and allow preparations to be made for working toward the desired situation in a step-by-step manner.

Operational management is also organized by creating a system in which problems are made visible directly, allowing immediate escalation to the appropriate level. One possible approach is to hold stand-up meetings, during which a daily state of affairs is discussed in 15 minutes: disruptions and problems are reported here. These meetings can take place at and between all levels of the organization.

During both the analysis and redesign phases, a great deal of attention should be devoted to training employees to use various tools and methods to make them self-sufficient for a subsequent process. This slowly embeds this procedural improvement approach into the company culture. To ensure knowledge and skills are and remain directly applicable, "just-in-time training" is preferred: following a strong

(Continued)

> ### BOX 1.2 (*CONTINUED*)   A "STANDARDIZED" APPROACH TO IMPLEMENTING LEAN?
>
> introduction, continue training based on concrete issues faced in daily practice. The real world is the best learning environment for Lean. "On-the-job-training" and "learning by doing" are crucial.
>
> #### IMPLEMENTATION PHASE
> During this phase, the formulated improvements are put into practice and redesigned processes are implemented by deploying improvements step by step, both within the process itself and process management. This is the most difficult phase because this is where real change happens and the potential for resistance is greatest. Getting through this process properly and realizing structural change in both processes and operations requires both leadership and persistence. Staying the course is particularly crucial at this stage.

The project plan shows up in Smith's inbox unexpectedly quickly and she dives right in—leading to her late arrival at the division department heads meeting. During the roundtable on current development, she tells them about her Lean project. A few colleagues are at the edge of their seat and want all the details. "Can we join in?" one of them asks. Smith explains that it is a pilot and the idea is to get Lean on Careville's policy agenda. "So I assume there will be room for it," she says, "but the budget is currently very limited." Her colleagues wish her all the best and want to be updated about any new developments. Fernandez, who is chairing the meeting, ends with a warning: "Make sure care doesn't suffer!" Smith bites her tongue. A year ago, she might have snapped back, but she is learned to choose her battles.

That evening, Smith reads through Quinn's project plan again. It seems eminently practical and hands-on and promises concrete results quickly. That appeals to her, but something's bothering her. "Can it really be that simple," she wonders, "and if it is, why do we need a consultant for six months?" She decides to discuss it with Quinn and Foster. She rereads the risks paragraph again, which does not say much at all about support and resistance. Plenty to discuss. She sends a few questions and issues back to Quinn by e-mail and calls it a day.

Before the project team meets to discuss the plan, Smith has a feedback session with Foster. She asks for his views on the plan. "Don't sugar coat it," she says. "Well," Foster replies, "this is the standard approach. That is what Lean consultants always do." "Yes, but do you think it's a good approach?" asks Smith. Foster has his doubts, but says he does not have any better alternatives. "How did it go at Asklepios?," she asks. "I'm not really sure," replies Foster, "when I got there, the first steps had already been taken, so we'd already passed this stage." "Do you think we could visit?" Smith suddenly asks, "I'm really curious to see what Lean looks like when it's been operating for a few years." Foster promises to send an e-mail to his former manager with a request and then it's time for the project meeting.

During the meeting with the project team, Smith asks some tough questions about the risks and how to develop a broad support base. Quinn admits he may have undersold the risk analysis. "Linda, could you give Quinn some input based on your experience with other projects in the ER? I'm sure we'll figure it out," says Smith. "And could you also consider what we can do to increase support among employees? Maybe we can assemble a sounding board." After the meeting, she takes Townsend aside. "Linda, I would really like you to become project leader on this. How would you feel about that?" Townsend immediately responds with a resounding yes, although she needs to clear it with her line manager first.

A few days later, a new version of the project plan is ready. Smith is reasonably happy with the result and thinks it is time to implement it, even though she has a feeling part of the story is still missing. Because of her full schedule and desire to get things going, she e-mails the plan to the steering committee and recommends a "go," as well as asking them to respond quickly. Torres responds almost immediately. He likes what he sees, but does not want to bypass the steering committee and will schedule a meeting in the short term. "If we don't consult them now, we ruin things forever, Jeanne" he says wisely.

Early the following week, the steering committee meets and approves the plan with minimal comment. Smith immediately shares the news with her "super trio," who respond enthusiastically. She decides to update immediately McLaughlin as well. He seems positive, but immediately says he really does not have the time to play an active role in the Lean project. Townsend is already discussing when they should schedule the first sessions with Quinn. They check with Smith and then get the proverbial show on the road. But that night, Smith lies awake, fretting. "What am I missing?" she wonders. She resolves to discuss it with Foster and decides to give Jameson another call as well. She is also not thrilled about the reservation expressed by McLaughlin. "I'm really going to need him," she thinks to herself.

Reflection

The starting shot has been fired. We see how the personal enthusiasm and courage of Jeanne Smith, fanned by her husband and actively supported by Torres and Townsend, looks like it will allow Lean to get off to a running start. Unlike most initiatives for process improvement, Lean does not require major upfront investments or expensive software. There is also no simple one-size-fits-all implementation. Support from the organization's leadership is required, but Lean can start small and grow organically. It is a good idea to involve an expert in Lean thinking and working during the initial phases of Lean. One of the key features of Lean philosophy is that leaders should eventually be developed from within the organization and not sourced from the outside. After all, you want leaders with a deep-seated understanding of working within the organization, who can live the Lean philosophy and are capable of teaching it to others.

Smith is dissatisfied with the current situation and wanting to change it shows courage. A good leader recognizes that the "drive" must initially come from himself/herself. Being driven is an absolute prerequisite. Half-heartedness is infectious and will be reflected by employees or team members.

Things are not going well in the ER, but Smith cannot quite identify the problem. Patient satisfaction and wait times are unacceptable. Smith feels a strong urge to address these areas for improvement, with a focus on the patient. Intuitively, this addresses the principle that Lean always begins and ends with the patient. Hiring someone with experience, like Foster, is a good move by Smith, as is the timely hiring of external support. The critical voices are currently silent, such as Morton and, to a lesser degree, Fernandez. But what will happen if Smith's uneasiness proves justified and opposing forces rise up?

Lean Leadership Attributes

2

Starting with Lean

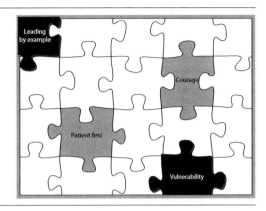

Before We Get Started

What Steps Should I Take When I Get Started with Lean?

Starting small with something big in mind. Keep it manageable and focus on the quick wins, but keep the next steps in mind (like when playing chess). And, most importantly, visit the workplace!

You should not try to do too much in one go: there is no point in training all managers immediately. Just-in-time training is better, that is, right before people start working with Lean. Hand-on training and learning-by-doing teaches employees new methods they can immediately apply to their tasks.

How Much Time Do I Need to Introduce Lean?

We prefer not to talk about "introducing" Lean: introduction implies finiteness, while Lean demands continued, persistent organizational change—there is always something to improve.

Who Needs to Be Involved When Getting Started with Lean?

Try to create a "vertical" band of brothers from the very start; a chain of leaders and employees from all levels of the hierarchy (board of directors, management, team leaders, workplace), who are dedicated to the cause. They will be essential for broader support at each level and to spread the virus.

Lean can only achieve long-term success if management at the top level is dedicated to the Lean journey and has established and communicated a clear vision of where it wants to go. You can start with Lean at any level within an organization, but constant and active participation is required from senior management if you wish to achieve results that extend beyond a few departments. People respond to signals they receive from leaders at all levels.

Case Study

Let's get back to Jeanne Smith's story. Thanks to the actively involved sponsor, the steering committee quickly reached a positive decision on the project plan. Smith's project team, led by Townsend, can get started on introducing Lean in the United Medical Center (UMC) Careville Emergency Room (ER). Smith is very excited and curious to see what will happen next.

This chapter introduces the following person:

Frank **Johnson**. Head of the Hospital Pharmacy. A somewhat worn-out man going on 60, who spends most of his time off reading weighty Russian literature.

Preparation Is Half the Battle

Following Lean consultant Quinn's recommendation, the first visible actions are a number of introductory talks in the workplace and awareness-raising meetings with the ER teams. Smith attends the first meeting and expresses her enthusiasm for introducing Lean in the ER during her introduction, stating that she has high expectations. She appears not to notice that the audience is not immediately convinced. Next, Quinn explains the core principles of Lean and how they will tackle the project. Townsend ends with a round of questions. "Will we be given the time for this?" asks an experienced nurse. "Why bother? The ER runs just fine," says another. "Start with the lab, it's chaos over there!" adds a third. Smith starts getting a little nervous, but Quinn keeps cool, even after someone sighs that this is probably just another way to cut costs. He explains that experience has shown that Lean almost always leads to rapid results that benefit everyone—not just employees, but also patients. The audience remains unconvinced, but appears to give the team the benefit of the doubt.

Resistance

Smith's schedule is overflowing with appointments, so she decides not to attend the other two meetings. When she cleans out her inbox on Saturday morning, she comes across Townsend's impressions of the two sessions. She finds an unwelcome surprise: there was much resistance during both other meetings and Townsend and Quinn found it difficult to keep things under control. She concludes that she should have been there, no matter how busy her schedule was. She sends Townsend and Quinn an encouraging e-mail and invites both to drop in quickly so they can discuss how to deal with the resistance. She also sends Foster the report, asking him about anything he may be hearing about the Lean project. After all, he is much closer to the workplace (Box 2.1).

Foster walks in at the end of the next day. He picked up murmurings, but there is no "war" going on yet. "Jeanne, I think you need to be more visible when we get started with Lean," he says. "Yeah, I've come to the same conclusion. Where's a good place to start?" she asks him. "You really should be at the first preparation meeting," replies Foster, "I think it's planned for the end of the week." He looks up the date and time and Smith notes that the session is scheduled at the same time as her meeting with Fernandez. "Bring her along," suggests Foster. "This is your chance to increase the divisional management's involvement." That seems like a great idea and she immediately sends Fernandez an invitation by e-mail. "How did that work at Asklepios? Did the department head also participate in the sessions?" asks Smith. "Yes," says Foster, "he was there more and more often. At first, he only attended occasionally, but later on in the process, he tried to attend about

BOX 2.1   RESISTANCE IN THE WORKPLACE

You cannot make an omelet without breaking eggs.

This expression clearly illustrates that resistance is part and parcel of achieving major change. This box includes a number of suggestions for turning resistance into opportunity:

1. Minimizing change is a common human trait. There is a reason changes in personal life—moving, remodeling, having a child, marriage, and so on—are often stressors. Even good changes are associated with stress. Keeping this in mind will allow a more relaxed approach to resistance in the workplace.

2. A rule of thumb is that the "A" for Attention is the reason for almost all resistance. Employees demonstrate their involvement by expressing resistance. By making the effort, they show that the (intended) change affects them. The least that can be expected in response is to take it seriously and give it attention. This is not the same as pseudo-listening and waving it aside, claiming "It's not that big a deal." A person who feels heard will be less inclined to hold on to the content of his message than a person who is ignored.

3. The art is to take resistance at face value, no more, no less. This seems obvious, but in practice, we often turn resistance into a bigger issue than it actually is, leading to the risk of overreaction or even escalation. Or we minimize its importance, with the risk of the other piling it on thick in response. The ideal is to find middle ground.

4. Consistently wanting to apply Lean principles means major changes. It requires a *mind shift*, discipline and persistence—major efforts from everyone involved. It forces everyone out of their comfort zone. Having a strong team in charge of the change can help a great deal, a team that can not only get people on board, but also keeps itself in check and on course.

5. Promoting participation, interaction, and communication is essential due to the impact and essence of Lean. Top-down implementation of Lean fans resistance and increases the risk of rejection reactions: "Not invented here." The risk of alienation is particularly high in sectors with highly educated professionals, such as health care. Processes that one has not been involved in are easily mistrusted or boycotted. This means that people are "included" in the why, what, and how along each step of the way, and given as much room for professional independence as possible.

6. Resistance is nurtured if management distances itself and fails to lead by example. This quickly raises the impression that the workplace needs to change, while management is—literally—above it. The consequences for workplace motivation are easily guessed. You can read more about this in Box 3.2. It is essential for leadership to be visible and available for promoting and representing the necessity, nature, and direction of the change.

7. Peers are the best ambassadors (*peer-to-peer*). A key success factor is to seek out employees at each level within the organization and use them to convince

(Continued)

> ## BOX 2.1 (*CONTINUED*)   RESISTANCE IN THE WORKPLACE
>
> others. This works better and is more believable than top-down communication and reasoning. Participation is also a core aspect of Lean. Working from ivory towers achieves the opposite of what Lean intends.
>
> 8. Regardless of participation and interaction, communicating "the Lean story" concisely and enthusiastically remains essential—not to ambush people with it at the drop of a hat, but make it immediately available when necessary. Any trace of doubt will be scrutinized and will tend to increase rather than reduce resistance.
>
> 9. The time factor: if we want to move too quickly, people will not keep up, particularly those who find it difficult to internalize new concepts or need time to process. Endless dawdling is also a problem, as we lose momentum. Timing and tempo—finding the middle ground.
>
> 10. Shared urgency: things are easier if "everyone" feels change is necessary. If "nobody" feels the urgency, we need to create that feeling.
>
> Smith quickly discovers the importance of active participation by professionals (point 5). She tries to organize learning experiences and moments for reflection—where she is personally present—to engender a sense of urgency and determination. You can read more about this in Box 5.3. Smith also strongly applies point 7. She also regularly reflects on timing and tempo in consultation with directly involved coworkers (point 9) in order to make well-founded choices.

half of all meetings." "What effect did that have?" "Well, the most notable change was that nobody dared skip meetings and everyone did their best to contribute something." "What did he do during the sessions?" "Nothing, really," says Foster "but his presence did change things; it increased productivity. And if a decision was needed, he could immediately make it or coordinate with division management. Oh, and he also played a coaching role: he mostly asked a lot of questions." They agree that Foster will soon try to organize a workplace visit at the Asklepios hospital, after which both head home.

During her commute, Smith is called by Quinn, who asks for an hour of her time for him and Townsend. Smith doesn't really have the time, but concludes that it is urgent and decides to make some time for the duo. Smith has a restless night and is at the hospital bright and early the next day. Quinn and Townsend are at her desk well before seven thirty. Smith grabs a quick cup of coffee and asks what she can do for them. They don't really have any urgent questions, but have a major problem with the resistance they encountered the previous week. Smith gives them a pep talk and provides concrete tips for getting everyone on board: it often helps to give people the time they need to express their resistance. A second tip is to have coworkers tell positive stories, not to tell them yourself, no matter how great the temptation. "Also," she says, "you can count on me for more support. I'll make the time to attend as many sessions as I can, because I think it's important." "Great," says Townsend. "That's a fantastic plan!" Visibly relieved, both leave the office, and Smith quickly moves on to other work (Box 2.2).

Townsend and, in particular, Quinn can often be found in the ER. They observe and talk to the team leaders and team members. They ask each individual about the key problems and bottlenecks and Quinn starts to form a picture of the potential quick wins. After a first round

BOX 2.2   VISIBILITY AND LEADING BY EXAMPLE BY THE LEAN LEADER

The leader's role is essential to organizational transformation. This is particularly true for the culture shift required to work according to Lean principles.

If you want to change people's behavior, you have to lead by example. This applies to both the board of directors and other management layers. If you want the people in your organization to improve continuously, you will need to give the right example and live it visibly and consistently. Everyone is familiar with the opposite: leaders who preach major changes, but place themselves above the law. They quickly lose goodwill and credibility and employees give up on the changes. Particularly in an organization full of critical, highly educated people, such as a care institution: *walk your talk, practice what you preach.*

Katzenbach, Steffen, and Kronley (2012) distinguish between two types of mechanisms that influence culture:

- Formal: reorganize reporting structures, training and processes, and so on
- Informal: leading by example, networking, *peer-to-peer* interaction, and so on

The reorganization of reporting lines and other formal forms of influence is easier and often safer to implement: the other needs to make the change and you, the manager, maintain control. Informal forms are not always popular among managers because they demand personal effort and often require vulnerability.

Introducing Lean places high demands on the (leadership by example) behavior of management, as Lean often requires that employees change a great deal and must be implemented consistently. If you, as a leader, say reducing admission duration is very important to you, but never visit the ward where major efforts are undertaken to achieve this, it indicates that you feel your own schedule is far more important.

Leadership by example and visibility not only inspire employees and increase credibility, but can also yield dividends for the manager. A lot of plans fail to come to fruition, with managers wondering why and getting angry because they don't happen, such as filling out forms that benefit the patient or patient safety. When you take a closer look, you will often discover that there are very understandable reasons for this. An example follows.

Everyone agrees that it is good for patient logistics and safety if a transfer form is completed when a patient leaves the operating room (OR). But this often doesn't happen. Actually visiting the OR and talking with those involved reveals at least two bottlenecks:

- Timing: the form needs to be completed when the patient is being wheeled out of the OR by others. Everyone is in a hurry, the patient needs to be lifted, and so on.
- The surroundings: there is nothing to write on, there is chaos, blood, and so on.

By going to take a look, asking employee questions and actually being willing to learn, the leader will be able to better steer the required changes. He can help resolve the (often practical) barriers employees have and show a desire to actively contribute to improving the primary process.

(Continued)

**BOX 2.2 (*CONTINUED*)   VISIBILITY AND LEADING
BY EXAMPLE BY THE LEAN LEADER**

Another example is that there are always people who continue to deny that a problem exists. This is an issue at all levels in the organization. Senior leaders sometimes do not want any part of a certain change. A leader must dare to intervene and indicate things cannot continue unchanged.

The urgency and desired behavior must be promoted consistently and demonstrated, particularly when it is difficult and people are in opposition.

If a department head allows one team leader to stop stand-up meetings and demands that others continue, his authority will quickly wane. This also applies to his own position. The regular stand-up meetings between him and his division managers must also continue. If his superiors were to put these meetings on hold, it would send a signal to the teams that they are free to stop as well.

The moral of the story is simple. A good example tends to be followed and the leader must clearly broadcast his willingness to lead changes and make them a priority. For Lean to work, the leader must actually be visible in the workplace, communicate directly with employees, and always act and think from the patient's perspective. He may show vulnerability and his own struggle. This will only make him more human and increase his credibility.

Smith notices that it requires a lot of efforts from her to be visible and lead by example at crucial moments. She still tries to continuously correct and improve her behavior.

of observations, they hold a meeting with a few of Foster's team members to prepare for the first session, during which they will chart the value stream. Foster is present, of course, and Smith joins in as agreed. Fernandez has decided to stay out of the picture for now; unfortunately, Smith wasn't able to convince her to attend. Smith also tried to get McLaughlin to join in and he seemed to be on board. Shortly before the meeting, however, he walks up to Smith and says: "I'm sorry Jeanne, but I have to leave. My daughter just called and told me she's got a serious problem at school, so I need to head there straight away."

Smith finds the meeting very interesting, although she's not exactly clear on where the gains will be made. When she asks Foster about it after the meeting, he explains the first step is to perform value stream mapping to get a clear picture of the process. "That will let us get a grip on the real problem as a team. The next step is to map the desired future situation, which will clarify the improvements that are needed, and to work on a solution from a position of mutual understanding." "So I'm too impatient," says Smith. "How did you think it went, Jonathan?" she asks him. "Not bad, not bad at all. The team was involved, I think it will go well." As Smith arrives home, she receives a call from McLaughlin. The crisis with his daughter has been resolved and he asks how the Lean session went. Smith briefly explains what they did and what the next step will be. McLaughlin says that he would like to be present for the value stream mapping.

A key aspect of the value stream, an area where things are not going well at all, is the delivery of medication by the pharmacy. Deciding to be proactive, Smith contacts the head of the pharmacy, Frank Johnson. That may have been a mistake, as she gets shot down. The ER never sticks to agreements, asks every question at least three times . . . in short, it's an extremely unproductive talk that, if anything, polarizes the relationship further rather than resolving it. Smith later talks to Quinn and asks him what she should have done. Quinn considers the question and responds that it is likely too early to work with departments. "It often helps to gently introduce this sort of discussion through divisional management," he notes. "But it is a good idea to discuss matters with the people we work with directly," he adds. "I think we can use our value stream mapping to clearly show why we want to work with them."

Working Visit

Foster has also managed to organize a working visit with his former employer. The three of them—Townsend is coming, too—travel to the Asklepios Hospital, where they are greeted warmly. After a chat over a cup of coffee, they immediately head to the ER—but the guests are given an assignment as well. "That's the way we do things now," explains their host. "Anyone can take a look, but we do ask for something in return. Please take a good look around and give us feedback about what you see. Do you see anything illogical happening or opportunities for improvement?" That's a great idea, thinks Smith—they get something out of it and we probably pay extra close attention. In an efficient 1-hour tour, they noticed a number of processes that are designed in a more clever way than in their own ER. They talk to a few nurses and one doctor, who are also very positive. "There's a sense of calm," he explains, "and patients are generally less stressed because the wait times are significantly shorter. And that's a good thing for both us and the patient. Smith and Townsend are extremely impressed and Foster is quite proud of "his" old workplace. During the feedback session, all three point out a few things they noticed to their host, who ends the session with a few enthusiastic tips. "Make sure you take a good look at the difference between leadership and management," he tells them. "You will need both, but you will have a greater need for leadership when you're getting started—meaning vision, guts, and attention for the why and the what. Too many managers jump straight to the 'how' by force of habit, and focus on minimizing risks. But no risk means no results." They eagerly ask follow-up questions, but unfortunately it is time to leave. Content and inspired, they drive back to Careville. Smith dozes off in the back seat.

In her mind's eye, she can see an ER without wait times, where smiling patients are treated by cheerfully whistling doctors and upbeat nurses …. Careville UMC's reputation in the area quickly grows and the patients start flooding in …. Thanks to Lean processes, they can handle the swift growth without too much difficulty. The quality of care continues to rise, costs fall, and productivity increases rapidly …. Other Careville UMC departments cannot wait to start working with Lean, and Townsend is giving tours to one group after another. Quinn now works full time at Careville, and Foster has been appointed as Lean program manager … Although she's sad to see him leave the ER ….

Crisis in the Emergency Room

And then they are back. While Townsend parks the car, Smith gradually wakes from her daydreaming. "Sleep well?" asks Foster with a grin. "Yeah, fine, now let's get back to work," she replies. Truer words were never spoken—they walk through the doors of the ER and into chaos. A group of elderly people feeling unwell after eating at a Chinese restaurant, two casualties from a car crash who came in together, and far more "normal cases" than usual. Foster jumps right in, and Smith gets a status update from one of the other team leaders. She tells Smith that several supplies had "suddenly" run out, that nobody could find enough IV poles and, to make matters worse, the x-ray machine had broken down.

The long wait times are driving patients and the people with them to despair. Now, hours later, they are slowly starting to get things back under control and the waiting room is no longer overflowing. As Smith walks through the ER, encouraging her worn-out coworkers, she is more convinced than ever that they need to do things differently. She decides to discuss the options for speeding up the process with her team. Maybe they can use today's experiences to hone their ambitions. She heads home, tired and more than a little confused—what a strange day, filled with contrasts!

The next day, Smith immediately schedules two meetings: one with ER team leaders and one with the Lean team. It's crunch time. No dawdling. Leadership is needed to show that she is serious about what is happening, and about Lean. Foster immediately suggests inviting the Lean team to the ER team leaders' meeting. "It's a great opportunity to discuss why we are so eager to implement Lean," he says. The meeting with the team leaders takes place the next day. Smith begins with a brief evaluation of the chaotic day earlier in the week. "Well," says one of the team leaders, "looking back, the main reason things got so out of hand was the problem with supplies." Another says it was short-staffing— he had tried to call in standby staff to no avail. A third confesses he forgot to check the maintenance status of the x-ray machine. "Basically," summarizes Smith, "we've got work to do!" She asks Townsend and Quinn to explain how they want to implement Lean and what result that might have. Everyone seems enthusiastic when the two of them explain their plans. But one of the team leaders lingers after the meeting and tells Smith: "Jeanne, I'm very concerned. Those two basically have no clue what goes on in the ER and how we work. And they're going to tell us what we're doing wrong?" And then she's gone, before Smith can respond.

A Lot of Work, Little Support

Smith spends the entire afternoon participating in the first value stream mapping. Unfortunately, McLaughlin isn't present—he's on night shifts this week. All of the participants—including Smith—are mildly shocked by the realization of just how makeshift and complicated many of their procedures are . . . Fifteen steps to admit a patient, and 10 phone calls to find a bed for a patient, to name just two examples. When Smith returns to her desk, her heart sinks at the pile of e-mails and callback notes. It's already five thirty, so she doesn't bother trying to call people back, but does process a large list of e-mails before she leaves to catch her train. That evening, she continues tackling her inbox until her husband says that it's eleven o'clock and that it's probably time to give it a rest for the day. "You're right," she says. "Let's have another glass of wine, I'm too wired to sleep right now." She talks about her day and confesses that she doesn't have the time to get her work done. "All this Lean stuff is really interesting, but if I'm not there, it hardly seems to get through to the teams. I wanted it myself, and I'm pushing for speed, but I get the feeling I can't keep up myself." "Just hold on for another day," replies her husband, "then unwind on the sailboat this weekend."

After a sunny, windy weekend of sailing, Smith gets back to work with high spirits. The crisis in the ER comes up again during her meeting with Fernandez. "Do you still have everything under control, Jeanne?" asks Fernandez. "Or is this Lean project of yours distracting you—we can't have that!" Smith wants to reply that it's also Fernandez's Lean project, but she holds her tongue. Instead, she explains they have already performed an extensive analysis and a report will be finished soon. "Since we're talking about Lean," she says, "you should participate in a value stream mapping. It's really very interesting!" Fernandez noncommittally promises to look into it. Smith starts to talk about the working visit to Asklepios, but Fernandez's phone rings and she is ushered out unceremoniously.

A Bit of Support

Before she returns to her office, Smith decides to pick up a double espresso in the hospital's main hall—she needs it after the meeting with Fernandez. As she walks down the long hallways, she ponders events. Fernandez isn't blocking Lean. Not yet, at least. But she isn't getting any support or being held accountable for it either. She hasn't heard anything from Morton since the steering committee meeting either. She decides to step outside to drink her coffee—it's cold but sunny. As she stands there, Torres walks in. "Hi Jeanne! How are your Lean plans developing?" he asks. "Well, first of all, I'm glad you ask," she says, "and as for how it's going? A bit slowly. I wish things would move faster, but I do think the understanding is slowly growing in the workplace." "I've actually been reading about Lean, and visited my counterpart in the Asklepios recently," replies Torres. "If I'm reading things right, you shouldn't worry about the lack of momentum at the beginning, that will work itself out. How are the reactions in the ER?" "Pretty good," says Smith, "of course there's always some grumbling, but I think we can keep them on board."

"Is there anything you need help with?" asks Torres. "Well, I'm not really getting any support within the division. What do you think we should do to get Susan and Cameron more involved?" replies Smith. They discuss the issue for a little longer and decide to schedule an early steering committee meeting. The first improvement meetings will have been held by then and Smith will probably be able to present some promising results. That might help. Unprompted, Torres starts talking about the importance of intrinsic involvement: investing in reaching people is crucial. "You don't need to get them moving, you need to seduce them into doing it themselves," he says. "It helps if you can present the potential benefits attractively, show everyone what there is gain and lead by example. It's about leadership first, management comes later. Have you ever looked at an overview of the differences between leadership and management," Torres asks Smith, "at how they need each other, but that it's sometimes necessary to focus on one of the two?" And then he quickly changes subject: "and let's not forget Kotter and get to work building a guiding coalition. What we need is a chain of supporters in all layers of the organization, from Patterson to Foster, a coalition of the willing. Let's make sure we also get a doctor and a senior nurse on board to connect with the workplace. And you can count me in as well." He's right, thinks Smith; Linda Townsend was talking about it, too. I really need to take a look at that book again.

Energized, Smith returns to the ER, thinking about how great it is that Torres decided to visit the Asklepios Hospital on his own, and has suddenly become her sparring partner in this Lean adventure of hers. The fact Torres knows his classics makes it all the more interesting.

Foster is waiting for her in her office. "Hi Jonathan, how's it going?" she asks him. He tries keeping a straight face, but has trouble suppressing a grin when he tells her about the improvement meeting they just had. "Tell me all about it," says Smith. Foster explains how they streamlined the registration process. The patient is registered directly by reception, giving the triage nurse immediate access to all data. "That speeds things up and prevents us from asking the patient the same questions over and over again," he says. "But that's not even the best news: I calculated we cut the time by at least a quarter!" "That sounds great!" says Smith, who is now at least as enthusiastic as Foster. "How did the team respond?" she asks him. "They're all on board—it was their own idea, and it makes their work easier," he replies. "That's great news!" says Smith, who then has to head out the door for her next meeting. On the way there, she walks into McLaughlin, who had heard about the fruitful improvement meeting. "I'll participate next week," he says.

When Smith participates in a value stream mapping later that week, attendance is low. Only five of the eight or nine expected participants show up. Smith asks those present if they have an explanation, but doesn't get much of a response. The mapping session is also disappointing—little is cleared up. She decides to cut the session short, much to everybody's relief. She asks Townsend and Quinn to stay for a talk. "What's going on?" she asks them. "I don't really know, no clue where everyone was," replies Quinn. "Is this common?" Smith asks him. Hesitantly, he admits there's often a relapse after the first two or three sessions. "It's as if the motivation's just gone," he says. "What do you think we should do?" asks Smith. Townsend suggests that Smith figure it out: "they can't ignore you and that will show them you're serious about this." Smith ponders this for a moment and says: "Linda, you're right. I shouldn't leave this to you" (Box 2.3).

BOX 2.3   RESISTANCE IN THE LINE

Every change is associated with resistance and actually changing behavior is difficult for people. This is true not only within organizations, but also in general; research has shown that only 10% of people who undergo bypass surgery make any changes to their lifestyle. Jeanne Smith is also noticing that two of her superiors, Fernandez and especially Morton, are not particularly inclined to change. Consistently applying Lean is even a challenge for Smith, even though she's positive about the principle.

A great deal is known about resistance and how to deal with it. Despite the best advice, more often than not, things go wrong when organizations change. This box contains more information about resistance in the line and how to deal with it.

The National Change Management Study 2006 provides a few insights into potential reasons for failed changes. Highly disruptive factors include:

- Employees in the organization feel management is unclear about what needs to change or improve.
- Managers are unable to clearly transmit vision and policy to their people.
- Management does not ensure that different parts of the organization learn from the experiences and problems of others.
- Agreements are not always adhered to.

In addition to a lack of clear and consistent communication, we also notice that people identify problems and negative developments, but tend to not do anything about them. Pfeffer and Sutton (1999) examine this process in detail. One of the causes they mention: upper management talks the talk, but doesn't walk the walk. These stories result in thick reports, programs and steering committees, staff and extensive management control systems, but not in the change actually required within the organization.

(Continued)

BOX 2.3 (*CONTINUED*)   RESISTANCE IN THE LINE

A commonly heard complaint is that upper management allows external factors to define its agenda, such as strategic alliances, commissions, and interests groups. These aspects are important to proper management of a company, but ignore the place where actual change is required. That needs to happen on the shop floor, where value is added and experienced by the customer. For Trader Joe's that's the supermarket, for a hospital it's the OR or the nursing ward. Many managers are (too) far removed from it. This increases the distance between analysis, vision, and realizing change. In such a situation, concrete translation of vision into changes for the shop floor requires an additional effort to get the people who need to do the work on board.

One of the leaders in the field of change management, Kotter (1996), along with many others, believe that absolute support by upper management, in word and deed, is essential for successful organizational change. It also requires a strong chain in the line and a consistent, clear message to ensure that the change cascades through the entire organization. Each management layer has a key role to play.

However, the initiative for change does not need to be restricted to the top.

How should you, as a manager, act if you strongly believe in Lean, and want to tempt your superiors to give it a fair chance, by removing resistance? Kotter identifies eight sequential steps to achieve change within organizations. We will examine these steps based on the UMC Careville ER case study to show how they can help reduce resistance.

1. **Establish a sense of urgency** Tempt managers to take a look at what is actually happening: how long patients have to wait, how much time it takes residents to get a hold of people in the hospital, to admit a patient, and so forth. Arguments that can be used are damage to reputation, financial risks, complaints from patient organizations, and so on.

2. **Create the guiding coalition** Try to involve at least one board representative and someone from each management layer below that. Use these ambassadors to convince their peers. This creates a chain of confederates who work on creating their own support, peer-to-peer. For Smith, Foster plays a key role in inspiring other team leaders.

3. **Develop a change strategy** This is about defining "true north" and formulating a strategy to work toward it, step by step. For Smith, motivating her superiors and tempting them to bear responsibilities at their level is key. If this is not (sufficiently) successful, she needs to avoid overplaying her hand and stick with her strengths.

4. **Communicate the vision for change** Understand what you want and explain it clearly, and link it directly to the problems you have made visible. Here too, Smith needs to ensure the right message is sent at the right level. Patterson has a different role to play than Morton, Fernandez, or Smith herself.

5. **Create broad support for change** See Step 2.

(*Continued*)

BOX 2.3 (*CONTINUED*)   RESISTANCE IN THE LINE

6. **Generate short-term wins** Highlighting these wins is just as important. More attention is often given to start-up meetings (when only an intention to change exists) than to celebrating initial successes. Smith can use these successes to create broader support and increase the sense of urgency within the organization.

7. **Consolidate improvements and achieve more change**

8. **Incorporate changes into the culture** These final steps can only be implemented at an organization-wide level, or at least at a level that surpasses the ER. This is illustrated by the course Smith's adventure follows.

The capacity to delegate is often—and justifiably—seen as an essential part of leadership, and also as a method to increase support and thereby reduce the risk of resistance. A leader must be able to trust others to get the job done. Too much or too little delegation can lead to management losing touch with the shop floor and losing the customer. This dissolves what the organization stands for.

Lean is all about managers keeping a close watch on the shop floor and the quality of the operational process. A classic mistake—one initially also made by Smith—is to place this responsibility with a working group and have the group keep the manager updated on progress and results. Practicing Lean philosophy and using Lean instruments are not things that are easily delegated (see also Box 3.2). All too often, leaders at all levels have become estranged from what they are primarily responsible for: communicating the goal to be achieved, organizing good processes, and promoting employee growth and problem-solving capacity. They often trust the management system to address these issues. This yields good performance figures, but the real problems remain hidden or warning signs appear only too late. That is why a Lean leader must go to the gemba (the source), and it is his responsibility to facilitate the solution of day-to-day problems through coaching. Smith does this by investigating the issues herself when value stream mapping attendance drops after initial success.

A Meeting with Management

Smith has a meeting with Morton soon after. He immediately asks about progress on the Lean project. "Show me some results, Jeanne. You've been at it for 6 weeks now," he says. Smith gulps and patiently explains the process they have gone through and that it will take some time for results to become visible. "But just to give you an example . . ." she begins, but Morton cuts her off, saying that a steering committee meeting needs to be scheduled soon and that he expects to see results by then. Smith says a meeting is already planned, which appears to close the topic. "Is the project plan still on schedule?" Morton asks next. "I propose we discuss that in the steering committee, where we will have all of the information we need," says Smith. They discuss a few more topics. After the meeting, Smith goes straight to her next meeting, with Fernandez. To her displeasure, the second meeting mirrors the first. Fernandez also wants to know whether the Lean project is on schedule, and when she can expect to see results. Smith can only just bring herself to try and motivate Fernandez to attend a value stream mapping, so she can see how necessary this Lean implementation really is. Fernandez concedes and promises to free an afternoon to attend—soon.

Reflection

We see the project to introduce Lean in the ER begin. Smith has noticed she needs to put in a lot of time to keep the process going. She quickly realizes that she, as a leader, needs to give the good example and continuously make her commitment visible. She does this by being present in the workplace on a daily basis to witness the process with her own eyes, working with the people, trying to understand the process and trying to improve things together during Lean sessions. That is the only way to figure out whether her assumptions about the processes are correct. By heading out and talking to employees in the workplace, Smith also shows vulnerability. She doesn't have all the answers and struggles with how difficult some problems are to solve.

We see Smith gain experience with one of the Lean instruments: value stream mapping. She discovers how this tool can provide a clear image of the current process. The scales often fall from participants' eyes when they see how few (necessary) processes and actions actually create value for the patient. Value stream mapping supports the visualization of more than just the single process level: the entire care chain and stream is made visible. It allows Smith and her coworkers to see more than waste alone. The causes of waste are literally mapped out and the value stream map shows the relationship between patient, material and information streams.

A key leadership role is creating an environment where problems are solved by people individually. Teach people to see problems by visualizing them. This shows everyone what condition the process is in at any given time. You know a problem can only be resolved if you know what the problem is! The goal is not to manage, but to teach. The workplace is the best place for this, not a classroom.

At the beginning of the Lean journey, Smith needs to ensure everyone is excited about the project. A good Lean leader involves the supporting departments at an early stage, ensuring the ultimate solution is a jointly supported solution. She needs to get people excited and involved in the Lean efforts. Conquering resistance among employees and managers is essential to the successful implementation of Lean. That requires effort. After all, a change in culture is required, where employees and managers work together to achieve a joint goal.

Keeping the improvement spirit alive is not easy for Smith. She learns to accept that she will be challenged again and again and is starting to realize the differences in performance are about a problem with the process, not with the individual. Smith first wants to improve the existing process before a completely new process is created. Improving an existing process means that you understand the process.

Smith's own managers hardly support her; Morton is not involved at all and getting Fernandez to commit to the project on her own accord is a challenge. Only staff director Torres openly supports Smith, and has even made the effort to learn more about Lean. That is a positive and encouraging development, but support and active involvement from line management are equally as important. Smith stays optimistic, although it is not always easy. Fortunately, the first concrete results are starting to show.

Lean Leadership Attributes

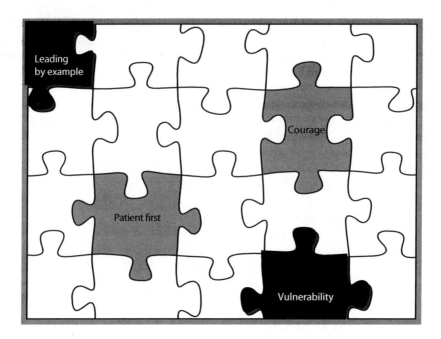

3

For Better or for Worse

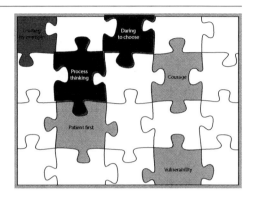

Slowly but surely, the introduction of Lean at Careville UMC starts to take off. Thanks to a few successes and a fortunate coincidence, the top of the organization is involved and enthused sooner than expected. There is also temporary resistance from management, particularly from operations. A key additional challenge facing the introduction of Lean is: how can you keep it manageable, since day-to-day activities continue and Lean demands quite a lot of time and attention from all parties involved, particularly those with line responsibilities.

Three weeks have passed. A number of sessions have been held in order to analyze the value stream and the first *future-state* mapping sessions have already been planned. Although the sessions are time consuming, almost everyone is enthusiastic; the value stream mapping makes it all too clear there is much to improve and the future-state mapping sessions present an attractive future.

This chapter introduces the following person:

Ellen **Kowalski**. Caring manager who shares her passion for health care with her partner, the director of a large home care organization.

Lean: A Bitter Necessity

Smith has headed to the work floor and asked people personally why they did not attend the Lean session. I forgot, I was too busy, and I had no time are the answers she gets. "I hear what you're saying," she replies, "but that's not acceptable: we made a commitment to this and unless there's a really good reason, I'm counting on you to be there!" Smith also talks to the team leaders involved to emphasize they are really committed to Lean now and that it is a priority. The team leaders promise to stay on top of things, but indicate they are sometimes shorthanded. "Good," replies Smith, "if there's a real bottleneck, come and talk to me, so we can figure out a solution to any impediments."

Care manager Fernandez has finally managed to free up an afternoon to attend a value stream mapping. At least, that is what she thought. The team is already in the next step—a future-state mapping—because they have already completed the value stream mapping. Fernandez's first impression is of a cluttered, messy board, but she keeps her lips sealed.

Smith comes in shortly afterward and welcomes her. Smith starts the session and a lively debate quickly ensues. Fernandez notices that everyone is actively participating and, to her surprise, even notices the junior staff are busy brainstorming. Toward the end of the afternoon, a kind of ideal image begins to form and she is left with the feeling that it is unfeasible, far removed from reality and besides, why is it needed? When Smith closes the meeting with a round of questions, Fernandez asks: "What's happening here is very interesting, but what do we need it for? The ER is running fine, isn't it?" Silence. Then one of the junior staff blurts out: "Actually, it's sorely needed. Remember the incident with the seniors from the Chinese restaurant? That was pure chaos and nobody knew how to deal with it." Others chime in to support her and Fernandez does not quite know how to respond; she mumbles something and falls silent. Smith silently thanks her junior staffer for the intervention and ends the session. They finish up with some feedback and Smith makes sure the junior staffer goes home with a positive feeling.

That evening, Fernandez calls Smith, wanting to discuss that afternoon's session. She understands that her comment wasn't particularly well timed and asks whether Smith can update her on the Lean project soon. Finally, thinks Smith, at least she is not talking about "your" Lean project any more. She promises Fernandez she will make an appointment soon and suggests taking Foster along so she can also get a view from the workplace. Fernandez hesitates, but finally agrees. "Ha!" exclaims Smith to her husband, "Susan put her foot in it this afternoon. But it's great she followed up immediately," she adds. "Managers ... " her husband responds. "It's no different at school." "Remember, I'm also part of 'the management,' Tom," replies Smith. This comment is the start of a serious conversation about what makes a manager a good "boss." Giving people space is important, as is listening and paying attention, they both conclude. "And actively taking responsibility," adds Smith, immediately thinking of Torres. "It seems to me that we're missing something," says her husband. "A good leader also provides direction and dares to make choices."

Box 3.3 at the end of this chapter contains more information about the personality of a leader.

The Workload Is Increasing

The rest of Smith's week is hectic and, much to her disappointment, she is forced to miss a Lean meeting. She is home late every night and goes back to work after dinner just to keep up. She even spends most of her weekend glued to her laptop instead of relaxing. The following week is not much better and, after missing another Lean session, she concludes it cannot go on like this. During dinner, she discusses the problem with her husband, who often has a fresh perspective on things. "It's no wonder you're swamped," he says. "After all, you only took on more work. I think you need to change something to make sure you can spend enough time on Lean." "I get that," replies Smith, "but how?" "Maybe you should perform an agenda analysis of your own work," suggests her husband. "That's actually a good idea. I'll ask Robert about his experiences with others." "Yeah, and ask Jonathan as well. After all, he also has a Lean background. I'm sure the managers there also faced this problem."

Smith is not the only one buckling under her workload (see Box 3.1). The issue is also raised during the emergency room (ER) team leaders' meeting. The team leaders state that organizing the Lean meetings costs them a lot of time. Puzzling out a solution to the tangle

BOX 3.1 THE LEAN LEADER'S TIME MANAGEMENT

Many managers experience the implementation of Lean as "a pile of extra questions and responsibilities." This is happening to Jeanne Smith as well. This is because Lean focuses on the issues that are often lacking from traditional management methods. Traditional management parameters are often focused on output: Are you staying within budget? Are you meeting your quotas? Are financial goals being achieved?

Lean has a stronger focus on the underlying process: input and throughput. The philosophy states that focusing on process ultimately results in the right output and a more stable and sustainable result than a direct focus on output alone. An example: a one-time action designed to achieve a cost savings goal usually achieves swift results. If, instead, you structurally improve the underlying investment process, this initially costs more time and energy, but ultimately yields a more structural and permanent solution.

Many schedules, including those of managers, are filled with activities that are not focused on the primary process, and therefore do not directly add value for the customer. Organizations demand this: working groups, accreditation, reporting cycles, and other such structures spring up everywhere. Meeting the corresponding requirements (imposed by others) often demands so much of a manager's time that the attention they can pay to their own process is threatened.

Such rules often result in window dressing—by all appearances, you (often temporarily) meet the requirements set without actually having to change, and without any structural change. This is work for the sake of work, and managers prefer to strive for structural and permanent improvement.

Lean places pressures on a schedule. The required additional time is not always supported by the organization and upper management. Smith's primary role as a manager is running the ER. In Lean terms: ensuring the patient is helped, without waiting or mistakes. To achieve continuous improvement, Smith will have to free at least an hour and a half a day to address practical issues and for other Lean activities. At the beginning of Lean, Smith notices that 90 minutes a day is not enough. Visibility (such as attending every Lean meeting) and leadership by example are necessary.

These time demands will raise questions among superiors, staff, and other managers in the Lean leader's environment. As a Lean leader, you need to be prepared for this. The challenge is to gradually garner support and backing from your own manager. We see Smith succeeds in doing so, although Morton is proving difficult to convince.

A key advantage is that focusing on the workplace and primary process eventually leads to time gains. For example, holding stand-up meetings every day can ultimately make regular meetings unnecessary. Most importantly, problems are identified and addressed at a far earlier stage, reducing the need for (large) projects.

In addition, Smith can immediately save time by identifying which activities she does because she has always done them and those that actually contribute to her primary responsibility as a manager, that is, ensuring that the patient is helped without waiting or mistakes taking place. Her husband's suggestion to take a closer look at her schedule is not such a bad idea. She will notice that certain activities are ritual rather than functional.

of shift rosters is a challenge every time. The sessions are also starting to cut into the time spent on the primary process. Those not attending a Lean session need to work twice as hard and that is becoming an issue.

"Right," says Smith, "what do we need to do to fix this? Because we're nowhere near finished with Lean, of course." Together they come up with three possible solutions: temporizing, suspending a few other projects, or temporarily deploying additional manpower from the temp pool. Smith thinks to herself: temporizing? Over my dead body! So she says she will ask for permission to temporarily draw an additional 10% from the temp pool to normalize pressures in the workplace. "That'll be a tough battle, but I'm in it to win! That should give us a little more flexibility for scheduling Lean sessions," she says. Foster, who has been fairly quiet until now, adds that the Lean project is starting to bear fruit and there are time gains; thanks to more efficient processes. "That should be noticeable soon," he says, "I'm seeing it already in my own team." His colleagues agree that something is changing, but do not clearly see any real time gains. Foster has a few concrete examples from his own team, which helps. "Now that you mention it, that's also happening in our team," responds one of the others. "Finally," says Smith, "I'm going to have a closer look at what projects we can shut down, temporarily or permanently. I get the feeling we're doing too many things half-heartedly. I had a quick look and we're running at least 12 projects in addition to Lean!" Smith ends the meeting and thanks everyone for their contributions. Foster stays on and Smith takes the opportunity to compliment him on his constructive attitude. Together they conclude that they need to make the results more visible. Smith will also bring up the issue with Townsend and Quinn.

That evening, Smith takes a closer look at the current projects in the ER. She makes a distinction between projects that contribute directly to moving in the right direction and those do not. Seven projects do not contribute to the final goal and she makes the rigorous decision to terminate them immediately. It's the only way to free time for Lean. During the course of the week, she talks to the project leaders involved directly and informs the team leaders in order to make sure there are no misunderstandings about which projects can continue.

A Special Steering Committee Meeting

Since a steering committee meeting is coming up soon, Smith has a meeting with Torres and Townsend. They take a look at the agenda and discuss possible tough spots. It all looks fine, although Torres says he wants to do everything possible to get Fernandez and Morton more involved. The meeting takes place the next day and meeting points are addressed one by one. But toward the end of the meeting, Morton cannot contain himself any longer. He sits on the edge of his seat and, in an unexpectedly cutting tone, asks when he can expect to see some results of "this Lean stuff." "All I'm hearing is that it's taking a lot of time, there are whiteboards covered in nonsensical post-its everywhere, and I don't see any changes," he says. "And I hear you've asked for extra capacity from the temp pool? That's unacceptable." Torres immediately responds with a question for Morton: "How have you contributed to the Lean project?" "Nobody asked me anything," he says firmly, "so I stayed out of it." "Well," says Fernandez, "Smith convinced me to attend a meeting. It cost me an afternoon and I didn't really understand what was going on at first. But it started to dawn on me later, once I'd taken the time to process it. You need more patience, Cameron. Consider it an in-depth investment. I really do see things going in the right direction."

"Yes but ... " sputters Morton, who is starting to get a little red in the face ... and the door opens and Bob Patterson, a member of the board of directors, walks in. Morton swallows what he was going to say. Patterson immediately asks how the Lean project is going. "I'm hearing good things about Lean from colleagues," he says, "and I'm given to understand there are fantastic things happening in our ER!" Before anybody can respond, Morton replies: "That's right! It's right on track and the results are great." What an opportunist, thinks Smith. "Jeanne, are you happy with our Lean project?" asks Patterson. "Yes, very! If anything I'm too impatient," she says, satisfied she is being addressed directly and, above all, happy that Patterson referred to it as our Lean project. "How about you, Susan, how do you think it's going?" Patterson follows up. Fernandez is also positive, but admits she is not entirely up-to-date on proceedings. "Well, do something about it," says Patterson forcefully, "you will need to be the beachhead for other departments." And with that, he is gone.

Smith suspects Torres of arranging this intervention, but he proclaims innocence when she confronts him about it. Torres does tell her that Patterson asked him to outline a path toward broadening Lean. "And I want to involve you in that process, Jeanne," he says. She's flattered, but her mind strays to her overflowing schedule, so she tells Torres she needs to think about it. "The problem is," she says, "I already have more work than time, and that's a problem."

Support Grows

Smith is not surprised that Morton wants to schedule a meeting to get an update on Lean that very same week. She tells his secretary she would be happy to, and asked to schedule a joint meeting with Fernandez, who asked for the same thing. "Fine," says the secretary, "but she's going on vacation for three weeks starting tomorrow." "Well, schedule the meeting when she gets back," responds Smith. "It can't be that urgent."

That weekend, Smith clears her head during a stormy sailing trip and starts her work week fully refreshed. To her great surprise, Morton is the first person to walk into her office. "Good morning Cameron, what can I do for you?" she asks him. It turns out he spent the entire Sunday in the ER of his home town's hospital. His son had been hit in the head with the boom during the first sail race of the season, causing severe dizziness and heavy bleeding from his ear. Morton was fuming—his son had to answer the same questions at least five times and then he had to wait, and wait some more, while he watched his boy almost bleed to death—at least, that's what it felt like. Hours passed before the surgeon finally had the time to put a few stitches in his son's ear, which took all of 3 minutes! In other words, he concluded, nothing Lean about it! "So I've decided we need to push forward harder, and I think we need you for that. I want to create a spearhead group with you, Luis Torres, a care manager—I was thinking Ellen Kowalski—and myself. Think about it. We'll talk again later this week. Sorry, but I have to run now, the supervisory board is here for a visit!" Smith is left flabbergasted, realizing she needs to tread carefully. On the other hand, she thinks to herself, this is the ideal time to ask for reinforcements—Morton can't refuse me now.

Smith realizes she needs to make some choices. Because she doesn't like dropping anything, she decides to get a few more management books. Maybe they can inspire her and help her make choices based on something other than her intuition alone. She asks Torres for recommendation, and he lends her a few books, including *First Things First* by Covey, Merrill, and Merrill (1994). "Browse through that and drop by next week to discuss it," he says. As is so often the case, Smith feels the support and notes that Torres mostly encourages her to discover things on her own. She begins reading that same evening. Her husband still finds it all fascinating and picks up one of Torres' other books. They discuss what they have read later that night over a glass of wine. Smith says, "What I think it's actually all about at this stage is leadership rather than management—giving people space and direction, encouraging and listening rather than guiding and controlling." They discuss the matter further and, before they know it, it is way past their bedtime.

BOX 3.2 MANAGEMENT VERSUS LEADERSHIP

In addition to the numerous studies conducted on the concept of leadership, there are almost just as many studies that clearly distinguish between leaders and managers. According to Maxwell (1998), there is a wide-spread misconception that leadership and management are one and the same. The key difference between the two is that leadership is about influencing people to follow, while management is designed to maintain systems and processes. The most disseminated theory is that leaders are visionaries and managers are people that get their hands dirty and the job done. After studying 80 chief executive officers and interviewing 10 successful "innovative" leaders, Bennis and Nanus (1990) wrote that leaders are concerned with the question of why the organization exists, not with the "nuts and bolts." Americans are underled and overmanaged. They do not pay enough attention to doing the right things and an excessive amount to doing things right.

Table 3.1 shows the difference between the two. Activities are often interleaved and both categories are necessary for the proper functioning of an organization. However, it is still important to understand the differences between and complementary nature of both, particularly when introducing a new paradigm such as Lean. Lean leadership is all about the extremes of the spectrum: leading in a visionary way and challenging employees to come up with their own solutions (leadership), while steering using strict frameworks, standards, and targets (management).

In general, leadership may be expected from the top of an organization, while management skills are found in middle management. A planning and management approach is not enough for the introduction of Lean philosophy and Lean leadership;

TABLE 3.1

Differences between Leadership and Management

Leadership	Management
Having and sharing a vision	Organizing
Focus on development/innovation	Administering
Communicating	Budgeting
Convincing	Consolidating
Monitoring	Planning and control
Inspiring	Problem solving
Mostly people oriented	Focused on systems and structures
"What" and "Why" questions	"How" and "When" questions
Doing the right things	Doing things right
"Span of support"	"Span of control"

(Continued)

> ### BOX 3.2 *(CONTINUED)* MANAGEMENT VERSUS LEADERSHIP
>
> leadership is essential at all levels within the organization in order to inspire employees to transformation and lead by example.
>
> Mintzberg (1973) identified the various roles and tasks managers must fulfill based on studying their activities. He distinguishes 10 roles divided into three categories, all of which require attention:
>
> Interpersonal roles:
> 1. Leadership role
> 2. Figurehead role
> 3. Liaison role
>
> Informative roles:
> 4. Disseminator role
> 5. Mentor role
> 6. Spokesman role
>
> Decisional roles:
> 7. Entrepreneur role
> 8. Disturbance handler role
> 9. Resource allocator role
> 10. Negotiator role
>
> One role dominates in each of the three categories, namely:
>
> 1. Figurehead role: the team explicitly contributes, but the leader defines and leads the way.
> 2. Mentor role: it is the leader's core task to help his people develop (themselves) in a mentor–apprentice structure.
> 3. Resource allocator role: in Lean, the term "heijunka" is used for the equal distribution of work over time and people.
>
> Lean leadership attempts to combine the best of both worlds.
>
> It is essential to dare focus on a target in the far distance: "the true north." At the same time, discipline and management tools are required to work steadily toward that goal.
>
> Lean leadership is "soft" and patient in the development of people and tough when it comes to following methods for development and problem solving. Bridging these extremes is a challenge for the Lean leader.

Townsend schedules a meeting with Smith and the project team. Townsend and Quinn report that the Lean sessions are becoming more and more productive, despite a few setbacks. "I noticed attendance is sometimes poor," says Smith, "but I respond to that every time, and get the feeling the message is coming through loud and clear now. I've also noticed we're ready to coordinate with other departments, considering the bottlenecks that are arising." "The problem I keep running into," says Quinn, "is that sorting out a bed for a patient during the night shift is almost impossible. I've heard several stories about interns spending more than half an hour on the phone before a patient can be transferred to the ward. That needs to be addressed 'upstairs' by management." "We'll get the steering committee to tackle that, since that's what they're there for," replies Smith. "I think Susan Fernandez needs to handle this. I'll make sure she's prepared. Could you write me a memo, so it's clear to her which departments you want to get involved? Oh, and one more thing," says Smith. "Looking at the value stream mapping results, we're coming up with literally hundreds of areas for improvement—some are issues that relate directly to patients, while others pertain to our internal processes. The issues are all valid, but it's much more than we can handle." Townsend agrees: "It's stifling and the list grows longer with each new session!" Quinn responds: "This is pretty common, even 'normal' during the start-up phase of Lean. I think it would be wise to make a few choices, so we can focus on a limited set of bottlenecks. We can broaden our scope at a later date." "What kind of choices do you have in mind?" asks Smith. Townsend replies: "I propose we start with relatively simple cases, broken arms, for example. They come in quite often and are generally pretty straightforward." Quinn agrees this is a good place to start and the decision is made. "Oh, and one other thing," says Smith. "How about coming out for a drink? It's on me. I think we deserve it after everything we've done, the project is going fantastically!"

Smith discusses the bed issue with McLaughlin. He is not immediately familiar with the issue, but he responds: "I'm not the one making all of those calls, of course. Now that you mention it, though," he continues, "residents do ask me for help quite often. When I call, there usually isn't much of a problem finding a bed for a patient. That's not a situation we want—availability of beds shouldn't depend on seniority!"

They organize a brief, scheduled meeting with the ER teams that same week. Smith once again emphasizes the importance of Lean and that everyone needs to be involved. "Yes, but ... " says one of the nurses and out spills a list of complaints about computer problems, issues with the pharmacy, and so on. Smith listens, and then replies: "Thank you for commenting. This is exactly why we need to start doing things differently." McLaughlin is next to speak: "I dream of creating an ER that I would like to be treated in. So what would that ER look like?" Suggestions flood in: "very short wait times," "friendly doctors," and "adequate diagnoses" to name a few. "That's right," says McLaughlin, "thanks for your input. Will you help Jeanne and me make this a reality?" The mood has definitely shifted. Though a few skeptics remain, the general feeling has shifted to "we're in this together."

A week later, Smith and her Lean team are at O'Connor's Bar and the mood is upbeat. The conversation shifts naturally to how various members of the steering committee are behaving. Fernandez is quickly labeled "nice enough, but a bit lethargic." "But she's starting to get enthusiastic about Lean and that's a good thing," replies Smith. She does not want to criticize her line manager too much. "Luis Torres, now there's a great guy," says Townsend. "He doesn't appear to do much, but he's very well informed." Smith agrees. "Yes, and he does a lot more to support our project and me personally behind the scenes. What do you guys think about Cameron?" asks Smith. "He's an odd one, isn't he? If it were up to him, we'd all still be using typewriters," responds Townsend. The banter goes on, the beer keeps flowing, and the mood continues to improve. The conversation shifts to Morton once again. "Cameron's quite a character," confesses Smith. "I really shouldn't be telling you this, but ... " and she tells them how Morton flip-flopped during the steering committee meeting the moment Patterson walked in. "Interesting," says Foster. "Well, he's all we've got!" replies Smith. "Guys, we need to get going if we're going to catch the last train," interrupts Townsend. She and Quinn say their goodbyes and head off. Foster and Smith order a final round and Smith tells him about Patterson's grand designs. "I'm trying to come up with a cunning plan because I'm going to need to drop some work. I barely get my work done as it is. We need to discuss that sometime, Jonathan," she says. "Any time," he replies.

BOX 3.3   THE PERSONALITY OF A LEADER

Many researchers and authors on leadership talk about the *personality* of a leader. In this section, we introduce a number of leading thinkers on Lean leadership.

Covey, Merrill, and Merrill (1994) believe that success is rooted in life according to clear values and standards like integrity, humility, respect, patience, and charity. Opposed to this is a pragmatic view on life that emphasizes personal performance and skills that help people achieve social success.

They distinguish eight characteristics of effective leadership. Together these form a developmental model for personal growth. The second characteristic is particularly interesting for Lean: "Begin with the End in Mind" .... Develop a clear picture of your destination. Lean leadership is about determining "true north" (an almost unreachable destination) for the very long term. In the short term, it is about targets that can be reached step by step.

Kets de Vries (2007) combines two approaches to leadership: the psychodynamic approach, which examines how people think, feel, and act, and the systemic approach, which is about the context (cultural, home, work) within which this happens.

Behavior often has an irrational component and unconscious drivers, with all attendant risks of dysfunction. Leaders must therefore enter into a dialog about their own "inner theater," as well as that of others: what motivates you, what moves you, and what influence does this have on the people around you? During an interview (2012), Kets de Vries summarized his "recipe" for effective leadership:

1. Good leaders deal in *hope*. They must be able to speak to people's imagination. This is consistent with "true north" in Lean leadership.

2. *Integrity*. Reliability demands leadership by example: *they have to walk the talk*.

3. *Courage*. To make decisions, particularly during a crisis. Lean leadership is about the courage to ask the question, to open yourself up, while at the same time/subsequently providing clear direction.

4. *Emotional intelligence*. Understanding what motivates people. Having a grasp of the inner theater of others and oneself.

5. *Self-knowledge*. Know your limitations and weaknesses. Seek out people who complement you.

Bennis and Nanus (1990) distinguish six basic components of leadership:

1. Guiding vision
2. Passion
3. Integrity
4. Trust
5. Curiosity
6. Boldness

(Continued)

BOX 3.3 (*CONTINUED*)   THE PERSONALITY OF A LEADER

In Lean leadership, trust is placed in the ability of people to develop and the conviction that errors are primarily due to the system they have constructed.

Bennis was one of the first to distinguish leadership from management. Both "roles" are required. However, leadership is more important when it comes to focusing organizations on the future and, where necessary, transforming them. A few quotes by Bennis, illustrating the differences between leadership and management (Bennis, Benne, and Chin, 1985), are given below:

- "The manager accepts the status quo; the leader challenges it."
- "Leaders are people who do the right thing; managers are people who do things right."
- "The manager has his eye on the bottom line; the leader has his eye on the horizon."
- "Failing organizations are usually over-managed and under-led."
- "The manager asks how and when; the leader asks what and why."

These differences are examined in more detail in Box 3.2.

The following quote by Bennis is a good segue into the writings of Collins: "Excellence is a better teacher than mediocrity. The lessons of the ordinary are everywhere. Truly profound and original insights are to be found only in studying the exemplary."

Based on years of research, Collins (2010) derived seven principles that distinguish "great" organizations from "good" ones. One such principle is "first who, then what": make sure you have the right people on board (and get rid of unsuitable people) before mapping the road to the future. Another principle is that great organizations have Level 5 leaders (as demonstrated in Table 3.2). These leaders bring together all of the properties from various developmental levels.

According to Collins, gurus with huge egos are not required to save an organization. Level 5 leaders embody contradictions: modesty and willpower, humility, and fearlessness. Level 5 leaders want their company to remain successful in future

TABLE 3.2

The Five Levels of Leadership

Level 5	Level 5 leader
	Builds long-term success with a conflicting mix of personal humility and professional will
Level 4	Effective leader
	Knows how to inspire a clear vision and strong commitment in others; stimulates great performance
Level 3	Competent manager
	Knows how to organize resources and people, achieves predefined goals in an effective and efficient manner
Level 2	Contributing team member
	Contributes to realizing team goals using personal skills; works effectively with other group members
Level 1	Highly capable individual
	Has talent, knowledge, skills, and a good attitude; is productive

Source: Collins, J., *Good to Great. Waarom sommige bedrijven een sprong maken… en andere niet*, Business Contact, Amsterdam, 2010.

(Continued)

BOX 3.3 (*CONTINUED*)   THE PERSONALITY OF A LEADER

generations and do not focus on personal fame. At the same time, it is important to realize that Level 5 leadership is not just about humility and modesty. It is also about the powerful determination to do what needs to be done. The strength of this category of leaders is that they use the so-called "window and mirror" principle if results fail to materialize or disappoint. They look out of their window to see what or who they can give credit to when things go well. And they look in the mirror when it comes to bearing responsibility for failure. They will never claim they had bad luck.

A true Lean leader is also a Level 5 leader who dares to think independently, does not fear others, and sticks to his principles: a visionary, steadfast, persistent, and dedicated. This demands a high degree of development according to Covey.

Jeanne Smith quickly discovers how essential and stressful it can be to stick to her principles and continue embracing them, even when faced with opposition. And how much support she receives from someone like Torres, who has a clear vision and acts accordingly. Combining these apparently conflicting traits, such as humility and persistence, receptiveness, and steadfastness, is a significant challenge for the Lean leader.

The previously developed philosophy of Greenleaf on servant leadership is consistent with those of Collins. Within this philosophy, organizational and personal changes are considered inseparably linked. Therefore, transformation is considered a collective, mutual responsibility. Service is the ideal tool for developing and nourishing care and quality within organizations.

This places the following demands on the servant leader:

- Leadership is a conscious choice that flows naturally from the desire to serve. It provides the opportunity for (also) serving in a broader sense.
- The primary goal is to strengthen the personal growth of others.
- This is not about power or personal gain.

These requirements apply to the Lean leader almost verbatim. We examine servant leadership within the context of Lean in more detail in Box 4.3.

Peter Drucker (1957) was writing about management and leadership back in the 1950s. We have him to thank for a sobering view on the leadership ideal:

> The most effective leaders I have spoken to and worked with over the past fifty years always locked themselves in their offices and were extremely antisocial. Some, certainly not most, were "nice guys," while others believed in strict discipline. (...) Some leaders were extremely arrogant without this affecting their performance, some were excessively humble without it negatively affecting their leadership qualities. (...) The only thing the successful leaders I have encountered had in common was what they lacked: they had little to no 'charisma' and were wholly uninterested in the term or what it meant.

Reflection

We see Lean start to gather momentum in this chapter. And the position and input of various individuals become increasingly clear. There are people who can influence success at every level, from high (Patterson, Morton) to low (junior staff). Some (Torres) provide support from the very beginning, while others (Fernandez) need some time to warm up and gain confidence. Jeanne Smith and her "dream team" have to deal with all of these differences and the opportunities they present. For Smith, leader of this Lean expedition, this sometimes means hard work against a strong current, a struggle that is sometimes lonely. It is important that she make the most of the "guiding coalition." This guiding coalition is currently mostly shaped by Smith, Torres, and, to a lesser degree, McLaughlin and Fernandez.

Their personal leadership plays a key role. Smith and her team are working hard to continuously improve their ER by looking for the best processes for helping patients. This requires setting a clear course and being visible in the workplace. In the meantime, the workload continues to increase and calls for corrective measures. Like Smith, who occasionally cannot decide on what to do next because of her overflowing schedule, employees also get confused about what they are supposed to do. As a leader, Smith can provide her employees with continuous feedback to make sure they perform at their best. But she cannot tackle everything at once—she has to make choices. She can and must also apply Lean principles to her own schedule, such as by setting aside time to work on improvements and carefully screening new tasks she is assigned. She will regularly need to ask herself what she will stop using today because some activities do not add value to her role as a leader. She also displays leadership by making choices and dropping a number of projects—and actively verifying they are actually terminated.

Lean Leadership Attributes

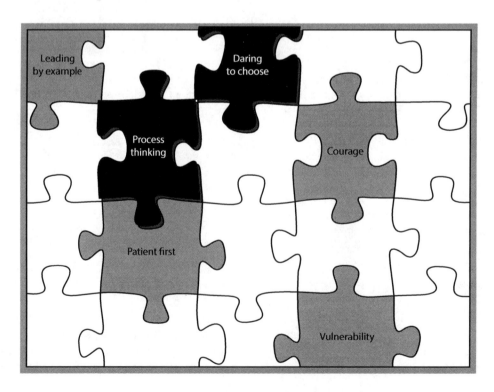

4

To the Workplace

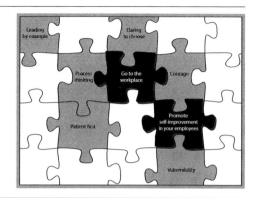

Case Study

The introduction of Lean is progressing swiftly, but requires effort. It keeps Smith and her team leaders extremely busy, and the time demands of the Lean sessions are also felt in the workplace. It is already leading to concrete results, however. These show the positive effect of Lean is significant: quality of care in the emergency room (ER) is increasing with leaps and jumps. This is reflected in particular by the average time patients spend in the ER: down from 5½ hours to 4½ hours. The number of medication errors has also dropped by 20%. Moving forward with Lean requires coordination with other departments—the ER does not operate in a vacuum. The first attempt—consulting the pharmacy—was a miserable failure (see Chapter 2). A careful approach is therefore required.

This chapter presents the following people:

Omar **Al Assaf**. New laboratory manager at Careville University Medical Center (UMC). An ambitious and intelligent young man with a distinct Southern drawl, at odds with his Arabic name and appearance.

Professor Peter **Jacobs**. Chairman of division management. The man is a brilliant cardiologist, but not always the easiest person to work with. He hasn't been working at Careville UMC for long. The Board of Directors is particularly proud they were able to bring him on board.

In the Workplace

As soon as Fernandez returns from vacation, it is finally time for the meeting between her, Morton, and Smith. Smith briefly outlines the steps she has taken. "And now," she says, "let me take you to the workplace so you can see the changes for yourself." Morton, who she knows never walks the ER, starts to sputter, but Fernandez already has one foot out the door. "Come on Cameron, this is going to be really interesting!" she encourages him. Morton reluctantly agrees, and once they arrive in the ER, Smith asks one of the nurses to show them what Lean means for his work. The nurse shows them two examples that benefit him every hour of every day. "Look," he says, showing them that the bandage scissors have been given a permanent place on the bandaging carts. "We used to spend all day looking for scissors, and ordered more new ones than I can count. There's no need

for that any more. It makes the work more pleasant and gives the patients a more professional impression." Fernandez is impressed, but Morton bluntly responds: "Is that all?"
The nurse is ready with a response: "It may not seem like much, but two minutes of time
gained each time for something we misplace 50 times per week is a lot: 100 minutes per
week, 5,200 minutes per year. That's almost 87 hours! And a pair of these scissors costs
$150 and we ordered 50 of them last year! Think what you like, but we're really happy
with the change, and it also makes the work easier." Morton says nothing in response,
but the nurse is just getting started: "The way we communicate with each other has also
improved. We understand each other better. We talk sooner, more easily and more often,
which prevents problems from growing out of hand and helps getting them solved sooner.
That's also good for patients, since we have more time to give them. All that thanks to the
daily stand-up meetings." Smith is proud of her nurse, who had the courage to speak to
his boss's boss. I wonder if he's read Kets de Vries (Box 3.3), she thinks to herself (Box 4.1).

BOX 4.1   LEAN AND TEAM RESOURCE MANAGEMENT

Care institutions are exciting in a lot of ways. Professionals work at the top of their
game, walking the fine line between life and death. Their actions are met with
increasing scrutiny from assertive patients, family members, and public opinion. No
wonder internal tension sometimes builds, tension relating to professional autonomy, power, and authority.

Team Resource Management (TRM) encompasses a philosophy designed to prevent errors and disasters, fitting perfectly within Lean thinking.

WHY TRM?

Fields including aviation have examples of fatal incidents that could have been pre-
vented if the (cockpit) team had functioned better. The collision on Tenerife (1977)
between a Royal Dutch Airlines (RDA) and Pan Am plane may have been avoided if
the captain had taken the questions asked by the first officer about whether the runway
was clear seriously, instead of letting haste guide his decisions.

Investigation and analysis of such aviation accidents showed that secondary errors
frequently occurred and one of the crew members (usually the copilot) failed to identify and contest the error made by another team member, usually one higher up the
ladder. Modern crew training therefore focuses on assertiveness and the capacity of
all team members to listen to one another, regardless of rank.

Studies into team function often focus on military or civilian first responders,
where command and control are essential to (military) operations. It is becoming
increasingly clear that the lessons learned there also apply to teams in other sectors,
such as health care and the (process) industry. Here too, teams work with variable
membership and errors can have fatal consequences.

WHAT IS TEAMWORK ALL ABOUT?

The acronym DAMCLAS is used in military aviation to describe the key skills of a team.
We will take a brief look at these skills, as we believe they also apply to health care:

(Continued)

BOX 4.1 (*CONTINUED*)   LEAN AND TEAM RESOURCE MANAGEMENT

1. *Decision Making*: Effective decision making; the ability to judge clearly and logically based on available information.

2. *Assertiveness*: The willingness to participate actively demands initiative and daring. Having the guts to challenge the team if they think something is wrong.

3. *Mission Analysis*: The ability to allocate, adjust, and monitor team resources based on the intended goal.

4. *Communication*: Not only sending, but also listening. To make sure everyone is entirely clear on what is happening.

5. *Leadership*: The capacity to guide and motivate the team. This is more than just leadership; it also applies to recognizing and utilizing the skills of team members.

6. *Adaptability/Flexibility*: The ability to make necessary course adjustments based on new information.

7. *Situational Awareness*: To what degree does each team member have a correct impression of their surroundings, of what exactly is going on?

Skills 2, 4, and 5 are particularly critical, as they relate to interaction in a context of authority. A junior team member may be right, but will he or she dare speak up and will others dare step off their pedestal and open themselves to feedback?

FROM TRM TO LEAN VIA COMPANY CULTURE

It may appear as though the skills described above can flourish better in an informal culture than in a formal, hierarchical setting, because it makes challenging and questioning each other easier. But that is only part of the story. An almost military precision and discipline is required to perform complex, high-risk, and safety-sensitive tasks such as surgery. Things go wrong if everyone simply acts as they see fit and each step is turned into a debate. Procedures, protocols, and conventions help to reduce the risk of deviations—and thus complications. There is a reason why the improvement kata (see Box 6.1) pays so much attention to perfecting skills and routines.

At the same time, procedures, protocols, and conventions also have risks:

- Being too sure of yourself
- Not allowing dissent
- Not seeing or not wanting to see deviations due to routine
- Not daring to raise objections out of fear of seeming stupid or simple-minded
- Not accepting any setback due to fixating on positive results
- Ignoring warning signs due to stress, external or group pressures
- And so on

Lean is also about discussion and investigating problems (deviations from the norm) as quickly as possible and at the right level. Everyone needs to feel free to

(*Continued*)

> ### BOX 4.1 (*CONTINUED*)   LEAN AND TEAM RESOURCE MANAGEMENT
>
> speak out, identify issues, and address problems. The leader's role is clear. He must lead by example: actively invite feedback, reward critical responses, and dare to confront others if they allow themselves to be lead primarily by power, authority, and/or vanity.
>
> Earlier in the book, we saw how a junior ER nurse dared to speak up to Fernandez after the latter had responded condescendingly to a successful improvement.
>
> We also saw Morton being berated by a nurse. Neither case is an example of a (potential) emergency, but leadership by example is threatened in both.

"Come on," says Smith cheerfully, "let's take a look at registration; a lot has happened there." The receptionist is briefly impressed by the "important" visitors, but quickly proceeds to explain how they drastically reduced the number of actions required to register a patient. "And you know what's really great," she tells Morton and Fernandez, "communication between us, the doctors, the nurses and the management has improved enormously. That's allowed us to provide fully completed charts much more often." Fernandez asks what they changed. The receptionist enthusiastically explains what happened. "We started by checking how many incomplete charts left here and looked at why they weren't filled out fully. We quickly discovered that many charts are filled out bedside, where there isn't really anywhere to write things down properly. So we installed a small shelf in each exam room, so notes can be taken during the examination." "Great, isn't it?" says Smith as they continue their tour. "And I hardly had to do anything, just listen to how the team came up with this solution and created a budget for the shelves." "You were actually at those sessions?" Morton asks, surprised. "Yes, I try to attend as many Lean sessions as possible. It shows them I'm taking this seriously and also lets me fulfill my coaching role," replies Smith. "No wonder you're so busy" is all he has to say in response (Box 4.2).

At the end of the tour, they talk to the on-call doctor. She says all that Lean stuff takes a lot of time, but despite this, she sees the added value: her charts are complete more often than they used to be, allowing her to work faster and significantly reduce mistakes. "The nurses really are much less stressed," she says, "and that makes my job a whole lot better. But what I really need right now is coordination with a few other departments. Getting lab results back on time is a major pain every time! I need to call a few times a day to chase them down and it drives me crazy sometimes. And don't get me started on the number of wrong results … We could use some support from you because we don't seem to get through to our colleagues." Fernandez is suddenly very quiet, but Morton says "he'll look into the matter." Sure, thinks Smith, you shouting at the laboratory head is going to help. And she immediately regrets keeping her doubts to herself and avoiding confrontation.

The next value stream mapping focuses on the patient with a broken arm, as they agreed earlier. McLaughlin is too busy to make it, but he made sure a resident was present during the session. The value stream mapping is quickly up on the board—the process appears pretty clear-cut. "Do we know how long this takes on average?" asks Smith. Nobody knows the answer. Estimates vary from an hour and a half to "probably half a day." Smith decides to experience it for herself and asks to be called as soon as a patient with a broken arm comes into the ER.

Later that week, Smith gets the call, drops everything and goes to the ER reception desk, where she is introduced to the patient, Lara. Lara is intrigued at being asked and

---

BOX 4.2   HOW TO TEACH PEOPLE EFFECTIVELY: THE COACHING KATA

The more actively and productively we use knowledge, the better it persists. Passively gathering information is far less effective than verbalizing it and experiencing it personally. And you only really master something once you transfer it to others. We therefore suggest not only reading this book, but above all using it and including others in the process.

We see that these principles are used extensively to enable effective learning: learning is less and less about consumption (reading, hearing, and seeing) but increasingly about exploration, production, experimentation, and using the material. Initial teaching is about integrated competencies rather than "bare" knowledge and, after school, learning takes place closer and closer to the workplace: the limit between learning, practicing, and working becomes blurred.

This development is consistent with the Lean philosophy, which can only flourish in a learning organization. Daily work is not only considered an end to achieving high-quality results. Lean adherents clearly view it as a means: to improve, to learn, to develop. The manager does not act as a traditional teacher who knows everything and occasionally shares that knowledge. The Lean leader is more of a coach who is able to place the initiative for development with the employee and, where necessary, challenge the employee to critical reflection and curiosity. He manages the techniques and instruments required for this process to succeed fully.

The so-called coaching kata (see also Box 6.1) is all about applying the master-apprentice principle, as is common in sports and technical professions, for example. The manager, as a coach, knows himself well and is capable of standing on the sidelines, letting go, and creating the necessary conditions. He resists the temptation to intervene, prescribe, and take over.

---

eagerly gives her consent. Lara is 26 years old and, other than her arm, in perfect health; she does not have a Careville patient card either. The receptionist is on the phone almost nonstop and it takes a good half hour to complete all the necessary formalities. The triage nurse is on her coffee break and only sees Lara 20 minutes later, who has been in the hospital for almost an hour. It takes another hour for a nurse to show up, who takes Lara to an examination room. The nurse does think that Lara has broken her arm and says she will get a doctor. The doctor shows up pretty quickly, conducts a brief physical exam and confirms the diagnosis. She writes an order for an x-ray and disappears after quickly explaining where Lara needs to go, more or less. Smith decides not to give any directions and Lara wanders around the ER for a while before she locates Radiology. It takes 20 minutes for the x-ray to get made, after which Lara goes back to the examination room. The resident quickly arrives and takes a look at the x-ray. She shows Lara the fracture. "A few weeks in a cast and you'll be good as new," she says. "But I need to check with my supervisor first." Unfortunately, she cannot get a hold of him and she promises to come back as quickly as possible. That takes half an hour and Lara is getting tired of waiting. She has been in the ER for over 3 hours now! And the pain and swelling are quickly getting worse. The resident finally comes back and writes out a treatment plan. Not much later, a (different) nurse appears and takes Lara to get a cast. Within 30 minutes, Lara has a solid cast and is sent off to Radiology for a check-up x-ray. Once the resident has seen the x-ray, another nurse shows up, gives Lara a brochure, and tells her to head out to reception to make a follow-up appointment. Reception is—again—busy, and 15 minutes later, Lara is ready to head home. Smith thanks her effusively and wishes her all the best (Box 4.3).

BOX 4.3   LEAN AND SERVANT LEADERSHIP

Servant leadership and the way the coaching kata describes how to lead are complementary. In this box, we first present the philosophy of founding father Greenleaf. We follow up with 10 ideal behavioral characteristics of the Lean leader. Finally, we summarize the relationship between servant leadership and Lean.

ROBERT GREENLEAF'S PHILOSOPHY

Servant leadership challenges leaders to increase all aspects of their personal effectiveness based on five principles:

- Personal mission: wanting to contribute and knowing what that contribution is.
- Connection: to be able to deal with dilemmas and paradoxes (win–win thinking).
- Idealism: daring to dream (vision) and converting dreams into action.
- Authenticity: being vulnerable and allowing intimacy.
- Depth: taking time for reflection and asking the important questions.

The goal is to support the individual development of employees and make personal power and gain secondary to that. Servant leadership is not without obligation, but focused on results and consistent with company values and integrity.

The strength of Greenleaf's philosophy is that it does not prescribe, but promotes thought. It places responsibility with you: responsibility for how you act and the choices you make. It stimulates self-reflection and asks meaningful questions, such as: why do I do, what I do, and am I doing what I want and need to do? It inspires you to give the best of yourself for your own development, the development of others and of your organization.

The first impression is that servant leadership holds a paradox within itself. Leaders should lead to prevent an organization from being pulled adrift. However, a servant leader does not allow himself to be pulled in an unwanted direction by the needs and desires of employees. He or she actively leads, but from a true position of serving others and helping them function and develop into the best they can be, with the aim of creating a healthy and successful organization. Anyone who truly believes that people determine the success of an organization must enable this, understand what motivates them and what they need.

RELATIONSHIP WITH LEAN

In servant leadership, leadership is subservient to individual employee development. This creates a nurturing environment for Lean, where increasing employee problem-solving capacity is so crucial.

(Continued)

> ### BOX 4.3 (*CONTINUED*) LEAN AND SERVANT LEADERSHIP
>
> The and–and approach is also shared. Lean also appears to combine contradicting viewpoints: the leader must provide space, keep a distance and then let go, while at the same time steering a strict course and rigorously applying the correct instruments.
>
> Lean means a culture shift and helps to support such a change. Leadership is an important vehicle for this. Lean leadership can be characterized as a form of servant leadership, without the two being synonymous. There are also similarities between Lean and coaching leadership. We address these similarities in more detail in Box 5.2.

Smith and Torres finally get around to discussing management theory with each other. Smith has been reading and was particularly inspired by Robert Greenleaf and his principles of servant leadership. "That makes sense," says Torres. "There are hospitals where servant leadership is applied and from what I've heard, it works very well." "What else did you find interesting?" asks Torres. "What I found inspiring and very recognizable was the distinction between management and leadership," replies Smith. "Ah, Bennis," responds Torres. "The more I think about it," continues Smith, "the more I notice I'm getting tired of the whole management stuff, while leadership is incredibly inspiring." "Why is that, you think?" asks Torres. "The best example I can give is how much the controlling way Morton tries to involve himself in my work contrasts with the inspiration you provide every time we meet," she replies. Contrary to his nature, Torres is visibly flattered. But he doesn't let vanity take hold. He emphasizes that Lean is impossible without management. "Vision and inspiration may be needed initially, but you've already experienced what happens if you don't stay on top of things as well." Unfortunately, the meeting has to end, and they each go to their next appointment.

Smith's experience with Lara's broken arm is the topic of their next improvement session. Smith points out the long waiting times between various steps in the value stream and asks the team leaders for their views. Together they conclude that it is unacceptable to them personally, let alone to the patient. They note that the receptionist spends an inordinate amount of time on the phone, meaning the patient has to wait. They decide to analyze the phone call situation to determine whether all calls are necessary or the problem could be resolved differently. A triage nurse indicates that breaks could be coordinated better, preventing everyone from being absent at the same time. They go through the entire process, preventing at least an hour and a half of waiting—on paper at least. In order to get a grip on the wait times, they also agree to record the time between arrival and departure for each patient in order to get a grasp on the average process time. Quinn draws a large diagram on the whiteboard where the receptionist can note this immediately. They allow for possible bias, as the patient may have been waiting for some time before the receptionist notes the time of arrival—accepting it is really the time the patient is registered. Satisfied, Smith walks back to her office with Quinn. "You're great at bringing out the creativity in the team leaders," she tells him. Quinn replies, "Yes, they feel safer if you set goals, and work hard to achieve them. We're making real progress!"

Beyond the Emergency Room

With the upcoming steering committee meeting in mind, Quinn and Townsend have written a brief memorandum, outlining which departments they would like to start cooperating with to expand the Lean process in the ER. They want to tackle the lab first: experience has shown that many urgent tests take three times longer than they should in practice and have noted that, on average, 1 in 30 analyses is performed incorrectly and needs to be repeated. They are sure that can be improved. They also want a dialog with the Cardiology and Surgery care wards, as getting a bed there during night shifts has proven particularly difficult. The last on their short list is the pharmacy—despite the disastrous response to their initial overtures.

Smith wonders whether they aren't taking on too much, trying to talk to all of the departments at the same time. "You're right, we need to take things step by step," says Quinn. In his experience, it takes a while before a department really gets on board. "If we try to steer matters a little, we can get it done eventually," he says. Smith is not entirely convinced, but decides to see where it goes.

Torres opens the steering committee meeting and welcomes everyone. Morton cancelled without giving a reason. "He's probably still hungover from the last meeting," quips Torres. When they reach the agenda point "cooperation with other departments," Fernandez starts looking a little nervous. Smith briefly outlines the proposal and then Torres says, "Susan, it seems to me it would be best to run this past the Care Managers. What do you think?" Fernandez makes a half-hearted attempt to shift the responsibility to Morton, to no avail. "Just to be clear," says Smith, "this is a matter of some urgency, so could you look into it ASAP please, Susan?" Once the rest of the agenda is addressed, they all go their separate ways. Torres asks Smith to stay for a moment and asks her to keep a close watch to make sure Fernandez does what has been agreed on. "And if she doesn't, let me know," he concludes.

Within the week, the head of the laboratory, Omar al Assaf, is standing in Smith's office. "Hi Jeanne, Susan asked me if we'd like to participate in your Lean project." "Our Lean project," says Smith, slightly irritated. Al Assaf is taken aback. Smith apologizes for her response and says, "Susan tackled that quickly. How do you feel about it?" "It's pretty cool. I've read a lot about it but have never really been directly involved," he replies. "I'm eager and willing to get started!" "That's great!" replies Smith. She tells Al Assaf that Townsend and Quinn will drop by very soon. To make sure things get moving quickly, she immediately sends the two an e-mail.

The head of the OR also responds out of the blue. He immediately asks whether he can attend a Lean session and is willing to clear his schedule to make it happen. Taken by surprise, Smith immediately invites him to the upcoming session, without really stopping to think about the fact the OR was not on the short list. She is pleased with the positive response, although she knows this will mean even more time spent on Lean. She finally makes an appointment with Foster to discuss reallocation as tasks, as they had discussed earlier—not that Foster has extra time on his hands, but she has to start somewhere. At the same time, Smith realizes she will need to find the time to coach Foster if she delegates tasks to him.

She also receives a long, but less enthusiastic e-mail response from Cardiology. The short version is "no time," though Smith feels the message really boils down to "no interest." The message isn't from the care manager, but from the department head, Professor Jacobs. Smith doesn't know him personally, but his reputation precedes him. Since the e-mail is addressed to the entire steering committee, she decides to wait for Torres' reaction. The initial response is from Fernandez, however. She has already briefly discussed the matter with her counterpart and they will talk to Jacobs together. Smith is impressed by this swift response; it looks like Fernandez is on board and starting to play the game. Smith also talks to McLaughlin. "Carl, just listen to Peter Jacobs' response," she says. McLaughlin shrugs. "Doesn't surprise me. We should sit down to discuss how to address that." Smith is also curious to see what surgery will do. As far as she knows, they're ready to try something new. She expects a more positive response than from Cardiology.

She's right. Surgery replies that they "would love to" participate. Care manager Ellen Kowalski says she wants to take the lead herself and immediately asks Smith for an appointment to discuss what this will entail. They schedule a meeting, which only appears to be possible in 6 weeks' time—both of their schedules are fully booked. Smith is secretly happy it will take a while, as it gives her a little breathing room. Quinn was right, things are not moving all that quickly.

The first exploratory meeting between Quinn and Townsend and the lab has taken place and they stop by to update Smith on what was discussed. "We walked around the lab and it was shocking," starts Quinn. "It's extremely cluttered and disorganized. It looks like it's easy to lose things there." "Actually," responds Townsend, "it's a fantastic opportunity, since it's clear there's a lot to be done." "That's true, low hanging fruit, ripe for the picking," agrees Quinn. "Great," says Smith, "so that's looking good. We need to make sure to initially focus on the value stream between the ER and the lab and not try to fix the entire lab immediately. What about Omar?" asks Smith. "His main point was that we need to take into account that a lot of people have been working in the lab for a very long time and are set in their ways. It won't be easy to get them to change," says Townsend.

More Success than Capacity for Action

A sunny summer weekend lies ahead. Smith calls her husband and suggests heading to the beach to go surfing. They agree that's a great idea and since Smith knows she isn't going to get any work done that weekend, she works late on Friday. On Saturday morning, Smith is dozing off in the passenger seat while her husband drives toward the coast.

Her mind wanders to the ER ... She is busy because the lab is participating in Lean, as well as the OR, and Surgery ... the pharmacy has a new head who also wants to get started on Lean immediately ... Careville UMC is abuzz and one morning, the illustrious maxillofacial surgeon Professor Reynolds is in her office, informing her that he will be taking part in Lean, it is of the utmost importance ... he owes it to his reputation, if only because he is the head of the world's greatest center for oral care! Torres is on a long vacation and to make matters worse, Smith's loyal employee Jonathan Foster is on sick leave due to back problems and will not be back for weeks ....

Smith wakes up in a cold sweat as her husband pulls up to the waterfront. "Sleep well?" he asks. "Not really, more of a nightmare actually, everyone was clamoring to participate in Lean," she replies, still groggy from the nap. "Well, you want to make sure Lean doesn't suffer from its own success," says Tom. They briefly talk it through, but quickly decide to do what they came for: surf.

After an exhilarating weekend on the water, Smith arrives at the hospital bursting with energy, muscle aches notwithstanding. She scans her schedule and decides it's time for drastic measures. The way things are going right now, she does not have the time to manage the ER's daily operations and the Lean project is being threatened. She picks up the phone and makes appointments with Torres and Fernandez. Torres immediately frees his schedule for her, understanding the urgency of her request. Fernandez is in Rochester for a conference, but has some time early next week according to her secretary. Smith runs into Patterson on her way to see Torres. "Hi Jeanne!" he says brightly. "How's it going?" Smith decides to be honest and responds, "Great, but with the ER and Lean, it's all getting to be a little too much to handle." To her surprise, Patterson responds with an "I'm surprised you've kept going this long." "Don't you have a right hand you can delegate a number of ER tasks to, so you can focus on Lean?" he asks her.

A short time later, she discusses the same issue with Torres. His first question is what possible solutions she has in mind. Smith responds with Patterson's suggestion, but Torres pushes for more, "Fine, but what about your ideas?" Smith sighs, "I feel like I'm stuck between the "old" world of the ER, where I have meeting after meeting and report after report, it drives me nuts. And on the other hand there's Lean, that all of us are pouring time into. I can see the benefits for the ER grow, but I'm not seeing that reflected in my own schedule." "What do you think would be required for your work to benefit from Lean?" asks Torres. Smith had already considered the matter.

"Actually, Luis, it may not be all that complicated. You heard about our stand-up meetings in the morning. That's starting to work and I may be able to cancel a number of those sched-uled process meetings. But I already know how Morton's going to react because he'll think he's losing control. I'm sure he reads all of the meeting minutes." "Doesn't he have anything better to do?" sighs Torres. "I also think I would like to give Jonathan more responsibility; he's ready for it and it would give me time I need for my own work," continues Smith.

Delegating and Reorganizing

The same week, Smith has a long meeting with Foster. Strengthened by Torres and Patterson, she explains her problem: "I'm drowning in work, I don't have enough time for Lean, and even routine ER matters are being left unfinished. I've thought about it long and hard and I always reach the same conclusion. I would like you to take over a number of my responsibilities. That will give you the opportunity to grow and me the space to take Lean to the next level. I hope I'm not ambushing you with this, but what do you think?" says Smith. Looking at the sparkle in his eye, she already knows his answer. "I'd love to!" he says enthusiastically. "I assume," says Smith, "that we should figure out what to do with your own responsibilities." "Actually," replies Foster, "I anticipated your question, so I've already given it some thought." They discuss the reorganization of responsibilities and agree to a handoff date two weeks in the future. Smith says she needs to coordinate with Fernandez and Morton first, but that shouldn't be an issue.

Fernandez is her next stop. She is a little skeptical about the plan, but understands the need and agrees. "Morton isn't here today, he's at a conference," says his secretary, "he'll be back on Monday." When Smith discusses the matter with him on Monday, Morton immediately starts to object. But once Smith reminds him of all the positive signals they witnessed during their brief tour of the ER, he realizes he is not going to win this battle. "However," he decides, "I demand that the weekly reports continue to be filed and I insist you personally run the weekly team leader meetings! I'm also still waiting for your input for the new quarterly report." With a "yes, I know," Smith hurries out the door before more bureaucracy is dumped on her.

At the end of the day, Smith spends a good hour talking to Al Assaf. He has been informed he has at least 10 FTE too many in his department. He's already discussing plans for reorganization with the Board of Directors and the employee board. "Jeanne, I'm afraid that means we will need to postpone our Lean plans," he says. "This is going to cause a lot of unrest and something as new is Lean is more than we can handle right now." Smith says, "I get that you're facing a major challenge, but couldn't we figure out a way to turn this situation to our advantage? If I'm reading things right, there are a lot of quick wins to be made with Lean in your department; if you temporarily use your excess FTEs to sus-tainably improve your processes, you can also reduce costs." Al Assaf does not share her optimism and doesn't concede. Smith does not press the matter any further, but decides to discuss the matter with Fernandez.

During the next team meeting, Smith brings up the number of meetings. "We have this meeting every week, and it always takes a good hour and a half," she says. To her surprise, the most senior team leader, the most set in her ways, says, "Now that we have daily stand-up meetings, we may not need that any more. Can't we get rid of the meetings entirely?" Smith is about to respond, but holds back for a moment. She is very interested to see what the rest think. Foster also keeps quiet, but another responds: "Getting rid of them entirely may be a bit much, so how about scaling it back to an hour once a month?" "That sounds good to me," says Smith, "all in favor?" And the decision is made. The minutes of the meeting are ready the next day as always and Smith sends them out by e-mail. Morton responds within the hour. "Jeanne, this is not what we agreed on!" Smith was prepared for his response, and says, "You're right, Morton, but do you really want us to hold a meeting every week because you think it's necessary? Because we actually talk to each other every day thanks to the stand-up meetings! That lets us change gears much faster," she concludes. She hears Morton try to think up a counterargument and a way to foil her plan and fail. "Fine, whatever, but rest assured, I'll be keeping an eye on you!" he says, and hangs up. Once again, Smith regrets leaving things as they are and avoiding a real confrontation.

Smith's phone rings. It's Torres, asking if she has the time to drop by. Not really, thinks Smith, but Torres never calls without reason, so she shifts her schedule around and goes to see him. He does not waste a minute. "Listen, Jeanne. Bob and I think we need to bring Lean to the next level in our hospital. Specifically, that means we want to turn it into a program with its own goal and budget and its own team." "That sounds great!" says Smith, but Torres is not finished. "And as far as we're concerned, you're the woman for the job!" He's caught Smith off-guard and she does not know how to respond. Torres waits patiently, interested to see her response. "You've caught me by surprise," says Smith, "but it sounds like a fantastic challenge." "Great," says Torres, "you don't need to decide right away, but let us know what you want to do by next week at the latest. I'd be more than happy to discuss the details with you." "When will the program get started?" asks Smith. "We're aiming for about six months," replies Torres. "That will give us the time we need to prepare and find a solution for the ER…" Smith interrupts him. "I may have a solution for that. With a little coaching, I think Jonathan is ready to take the next step and that will put a 'believer' in that spot. That's essential for success, I think." Torres hadn't considered that yet and the idea appeals to him. "But I really have to run to my next meeting," says Smith, "I'll get back to you next week."

Everything is changing rapidly from there on out. Smith has already made her decision when she discusses the offer with her husband. He's proud of her, pushing her to say "yes." A few days later, Smith is meeting with Patterson and Torres to do a bit of brainstorming. When the meeting is finally over, Patterson says, "Jeanne, I've got an interesting opportunity for you. I've got contacts in the Robert Kennedy Hospital in Oregon and they're willing to have you work in their Lean program for a month. Consider it a kind of internship. They're quite far along already, so we could learn a lot from them. We'll visit with a delegation from Careville toward the end of your stay there to get a feeling for what you've learned." Smith is surprised and overjoyed.

Once she's settled down a little, she heads off to see Fernandez to discuss the reorganization in the lab. Fernandez has done her homework and has already had extensive talks with Al Assaf's manager. "It took a lot of talking, but we've hammered out an agreement," says Fernandez. "We also talked to Omar and he's been given some wiggle room to make the transition, so that you can start working on streamlining cooperation between the ER and lab together." "That's fantastic!" says Smith.

Reflection

In this chapter, we witness how Morton's management style is increasingly at odds with Torres' involved, coaching approach. Smith fights to follow her own course in spite of him, with increasing support from Fernandez, though the latter is still keeping a low profile. Smith is discovering that Torres' leadership style also suits her and we see her begin to support her team leaders in a similar manner. Almost unnoticed, this is the beginning of a culture shift within Careville UMC. At the same time, Smith is letting opportunities slip past by resisting Morton without actually confronting him or addressing the conflict in greater depth. Even though Morton is her superior, as a Lean leader, she could take the initiative herself.

We see Smith take her superiors into the workplace, where they are literally surprised by everything that is happening there. This situation clearly illustrates the importance of looking around in the workplace: a lot of what goes on there is invisible from a manager's office. It is almost impossible to directly support your employees with the practical issues they face day in and day out, from that ivory tower.

The road to Lean is still littered with obstacles—as they attempt to expand beyond the ER, they are faced with various forms of resistance as well as department heads who want to dive in head first. Keeping a handle on the situation is a real challenge. It is very important to steer a clear course and make the right choices. Within this context, Smith's offer to the head of the OR to join in is a course deviation, as that department was not on the initial short list.

Lean Leadership Attributes

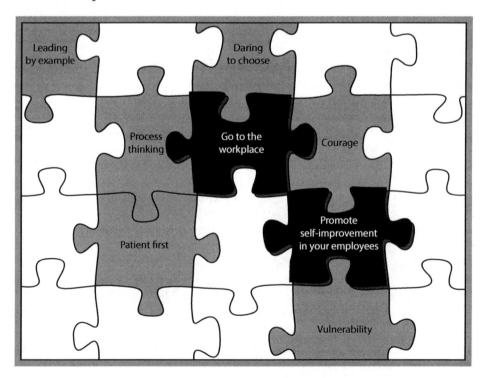

5

An Inspiring Internship

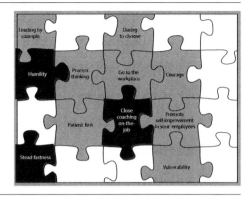

Case Study

The clock is ticking, and just before Smith heads off to Oregon, she hands over her responsibilities to Foster, who will take over running the emergency room (ER) in her absence. They have agreed that Foster will focus on the "regular" work, which will likely keep him busy enough. This means further implementation of Lean will temporarily be a lower priority—there's no way around it.

This chapter introduces the following people, all of whom work at the Robert Kennedy Hospital (RKH), where Smith will intern for 4 weeks:

- Agnes **Karlsson**. Lean program manager. Set up the Lean program and has been leading it successfully for the past 3 years, but is eagerly looking for the next step.
- Margo **Davidson**. Strategy and Policy Director. Comes from a rich family, with a beautiful house on the coast where she enjoys entertaining colleagues and other guests.
- Ingrid **Pearson**. Member of the Board of Directors and a close colleague of Bob Patterson. She has only been at the RKH for 2 years and is a strong proponent of the Lean philosophy.
- Eric **Taylor**. Head of the ER, die-hard Lean adherent.
- Jacob **Vargas**. Human Resource (HR) Director. Perfect example of a servant leader.

The First Week

After a relaxing week of holiday exploring the Pacific Northwest, Smith reports for duty at the RKH. Her host, Agnes Karlsson welcomes her, and after a chat and a cup of coffee, takes her on a brief tour and gets things moving. They have made all the necessary preparations in advance by e-mail and Skype, so little introduction is needed. The core of Smith's "internship assignment" is to develop a plan for the next stage in Lean at the RKH. Karlsson has an urgent need for that, because she has the feeling Lean has been standing still ever since lasting successes were achieved during a previous phase. "All of the low hanging fruit has been harvested," says Karlsson, "but that doesn't mean we're done. There's still ample room for improvement, particularly in processes that extend beyond departmental borders." "What does your true north look like," asks Smith. Karlsson succinctly summarizes the true north of the RKH: patient satisfaction of at least 8/10, getting rid of all admission days that are not medically required, and an outpatient clinic wait time of no more than 10 minutes.

The second assignment Smith has set herself is to investigate leadership at the RKH. She wants to eventually be able to provide guidance and support in that area from the program office. Karlsson has a whole schedule laid for Smith, detailing who she will talk to and what sessions she can join. The first day is a blur, and Smith is invited to Karlsson's house for dinner that evening. During dinner, Karlsson's husband—an engineer for a large company—shares a few juicy stories about his manager. "Today, for example, he suddenly wanted me to tell him how many people will get training next year," he says, "even though we'd just agreed that HR was going to create an integrated training curriculum!" It is a great evening, filled with mirth and laughter. After dinner, over coffee, she is calmed down and thinks about the stories: "That's really a classic example of management behavior, no leadership to be seen." Karlsson agrees immediately and adds they unfortunately still have a few of those people skulking around her hospital. "And they're a thorn in my side," she concludes.

Smith spends the entire week in the workplace. She talks to people at all levels, and she is impressed. Everywhere she goes, "something" is being done with Lean, and everyone she talks to seems to know what it's all about. On Friday afternoon, she has a long talk with Karlsson, who asks her about what she's noticed. Smith provides examples, such as fewer hospital days, fewer medication errors and time spent looking for materials, and that employees document improvements in a structured manner. Karlsson and Smith really get into it. "Why do you think Lean is stagnating, Agnes?" asks Smith. "Looking at how things are going, it seems to me everyone is actively involved, and I've noticed the Lean tools are being used everywhere." "Well, yes," replies Karlsson, "but I'm convinced there's more to be gained. We've more or less achieved our program goals, which is exactly why I need a plan for the next step. There's a reason we refer to 'kaizen', I want to keep making things better." "Have you already reached true north?" asks Smith. "The fact you need ask means you've got an answer," retorts Karlsson, "so no, we certainly haven't reached it yet. I think our best bet is focusing on Leader Standard Work." "OK," replies Smith, "I'll take that on board." (See Box 5.1)

BOX 5.1   LEADER STANDARD WORK

A key Lean principle is that focusing on the process automatically leads to results. This does mean the process requires active steering. This is a key responsibility for the leader. "Leader Standard Work" (LSW) documents what the leader strives for, how and when he does that, and how the leader responds to problems. This box contains more about LSW within the context of Lean management and in relation to traditional management.

TRADITIONAL MANAGEMENT

More traditional forms of management are primarily focused on staying on schedule and budget. Managers are expected to deploy *ad hoc* solutions if this is required to stay on schedule. It is always all about hitting the numbers.

(Continued)

BOX 5.1 (*CONTINUED*)   LEADER STANDARD WORK

Traditional management also frequently uses structured processes to make day-to-day problems disappear or at least diminish. Many meetings, phone calls, and e-mails are focused on running daily operations. The manager plans the results, but usually delegates the process to the employees. He therefore spends a lot of time in his office and in meetings, reads reports and spreadsheets, and adjusts course if results are not where they should be.

LEAN MANAGEMENT

In Lean management, the primary focus is on maintaining and improving processes. Managers are expected to understand and eliminate the source of problems. The central issue is always: "What caused the problem which disrupted the process and who is doing what to resolve it?"

This means many structured processes are designed to make problems visible and remove the root cause thereof. The manager plans the process and the results. He spends a lot of time in the workplace and makes adjustments if the process is not as desired.

LEADER STANDARD WORK

This is about actively managing the process. This is done using a kind of meta-process, which can be used to manage our processes in the here and now. The Japanese call this "genchi genbutsu," managing where it is actually happening: the actual place, the actual process, the actual product. The golden rule: always look and experience for yourself. This is the only way to check your assumptions and identify the true problems.

What does LSW mean in concrete terms?

1. It is an overview of standard tasks required to maintain the Lean management system, such as workplace visits, (daily) meetings and improvement activities.
2. It also documents how long something should last and how often it should be done.
3. Focus on the primary process.
4. The primary process focuses the leader on checking visual signals and checks.
5. It continuously develops and improves itself, documenting current Lean management best practices. It thus provides the foundation for further improvement to the Lean management system.

LEADER STANDARD WORK IN HEALTH CARE

LSW clearly documents the Lean management system. It provides clarity regarding the behavior expected from managers: what should they do?

LSW in a Lean care institution is focused on the needs of patients and strives to improve the quality of care. This is done by, for example, reducing process times, eliminating errors, speeding up delivery, and placing activities that add value for the patient first.

That weekend, Smith takes a long kayak through the sounds. While enjoying the scenery and the peace and quiet, she ponders everything she has experienced over the past week. The thing that probably struck her the most was the calm in all the departments—she literally had not seen anybody looking for anything. Patients and the people accompanying them also appeared to know where they were going. That is different back home, she sighs, where we're always losing something—sometimes even patients!—enough to drive a person crazy. She decides to ask Karlsson if the claim she noticed was there before, or whether it was an effect of Lean. She doesn't have a clear view of her other area of interest, leadership. She did notice Board of Directors member Ingrid Pearson was very pleasant to work with and had an almost coaching approach to answering her questions, instead of providing quick responses. The fact they had met in the workplace rather than in the Board of Directors offices was also interesting. That's not something she thought Patterson would do, let alone someone like Cameron Morton. Pearson had shown her how she managed to help resolve a notorious bottleneck between the ER and the pharmacy: there was an insurmountable manpower issue in the pharmacy, she said, and she had freed budget to address the issue immediately. (See Box 5.2)

BOX 5.2   COACHING LEADERSHIP

"You cannot teach a man anything, you can only help to discover it within himself."
—Galileo Galilei

At Toyota, coaching is an essential management task. Everyone is responsible for developing his own people and also has their own coach for personal development. In this box, we present the principles of coaching leadership and the associated improvement kata.

What the coaching process looks like is described in detail in the book *Toyota Kata* (2009) by Mike Rother. The development culture within Toyota is similar to a master–apprentice structure as found in medieval guilds. The goal is for the coachee to learn to improve: not in the classroom, based on books or instruction, but by doing it himself. The role of the coach is to allow the coachee to discover how to find solutions to problems on his own. The idea *is* for the coach to lead by example and mirror desirable behavior, but *not* to take finding the solution away from the apprentice or take over the apprentice's desired behavior. Therein lies a difference with the guild era, in which demonstration and imitation were common.

This coaching process is called the improvement kata. Five questions lie at its heart:

1. What is the current situation?
2. What is the desired situation?
3. What obstacles are standing in the way?
4. What is your next step?
5. When can we look at the result and at what we have learned?

By consistently asking these questions, the coach allows the "apprentice" to experiment to find solutions. This is fundamentally different from the current practice within many organizations. All too often, a bottleneck is analyzed and a decision is made about what needs to be done better, and the employee gets to work based on a

(Continued)

BOX 5.2 (*CONTINUED*)   COACHING LEADERSHIP

plan. Whether the employee is on course or adjustments are necessary is determined during six-month or annual performance reviews. In this process, managers ignore the fact that individual knowledge and situations are subject to continuous change, employees are insufficiently able to experiment, learn, and adapt, or only able to do so occasionally. This is also reflected by the fact managers stop employees or change their approach to working toward improvement if success isn't swift enough, instead of exploring and making the most of the learning situation. Applying the improvement kata teaches the apprentice to explore, test, adjust, and perfect lasting solutions on his own. This is better and more sustainable than applying (short-term) solutions thought up by others. The apprentice takes center stage instead of being the extension of his superiors, the subject rather than the object.

Rother: "With the improvement kata you work step-by-step toward a challenging target condition, learning along the way. You work on those things you discover you *need* to work on to reach your objective." This is demonstrated in Figure 5.1.

Coaching using the improvement kata is similar to training athletes: standing by the sidelines; watching what they do, preferably every day; coaching on-the-job. This is a continuous process that occurs on all levels, not by taking things over or modeling them (let me kick the ball just this once), but by helping the apprentice examine, test and strengthen his own problem solving skills.

This is fundamentally different from the approach common to many organizations outside of sport, where coaching discussion occur only sporadically, and where a manager letting his professionals go is considered a sign of trust and freedom. This is associated with a significant risk of neglecting the leader's role as a coach. In recent years, the "professional independence" of professionals has sometimes been limited by technocratic managers who—armed with spreadsheets and procedures—attempted to dictate *what* they needed to and *how* it needed to be done. This resulted in reactionary movements calling for greater personal responsibility and autonomy,

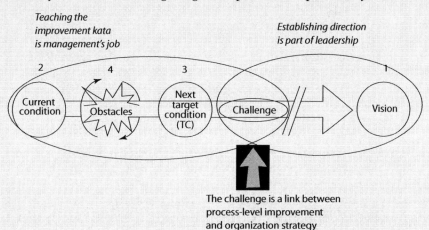

FIGURE 5.1

A schematic representation of the improvement kata. (Redrawn from Rother, M., *Toyota Kata. Managing People for Continuous Improvement and Superior Results*, McGraw-Hill, New York, 2009.)

(Continued)

BOX 5.2 (*CONTINUED*)   COACHING LEADERSHIP

and less paternalism: "Managing professionals? Don't do it!" (Weggeman, 2008). The alluring conclusion that might be drawn from this is that the manager should avoid all involvement. "Tell the professional what you expect from him, but don't bother him with the how." In the improvement kata, the manager keeps a distance from a great deal of things, but explicitly not from the employee's development *process*. He supports this on a daily basis, without a patronizing attitude in terms of content.

The greatest challenge during the enormous growth Toyota experienced during the past few decades was the ability to expand the number of coaches without negatively influencing the layer below. Standard practice is that one must have at least 10 years of experience with the improvement kata before being able to provide strong, independent coaching using it. Two things make coaching at Toyota powerful and unique: the intensity and the structured approach that result from consistently applying the improvement kata.

We examine the improvement kata and associated coaching kata in greater detail in a separate in-depth Box 6.1.

In Oregon, Smith is discovering she has a lot to learn from managers for whom coaching has become second nature, such as Pearson and Davidson.

Week Two

During the second week, Smith is making more rounds through the RKH and meets more new people. She attends at least one stand-up meeting and one 5S meeting each day. Once she has gotten used to the way things work here in Oregon, she also chips in. Her active input is valued and the head of the ER, Eric Taylor, asks if she can come back a few times. "It's great to have a fresh perspective on what we're doing, it's extremely helpful." Smith is happy to, and makes an appointment to have lunch together to talk things through in an informal setting. During the course of the second week, Smith also meets with the Strategy and Policy director, Margo Davidson. Once again, she's struck by the respectful attitude. Smith and Davidson discuss where the RKH hospital is headed, and how Lean contributes to its strategic goals. And while Davidson may not seem to share much with Torres at first glance, Smith notices the same coaching attitude she values so highly in her own Strategy and Policy director. The focused, decisive attitude is also something both share. She decides to ask about that: "What are your views on the management style here, and is it something you're actively involved in?" Davidson's reaction is hardly a surprise: "We started focusing on *servant leadership* a few years back, and we've been actively attempting to root out "classic" management behavior since. That's sorely needed, because we've noticed time and again that directive, controlling management combines poorly with Lean. That doesn't mean there isn't any control anymore, but it's no longer control for its own sake. Since we decided to go with Lean, discussing management style with our managers quickly became a key part of our change strategy. I must admit, things didn't always go smoothly. Several managers left, because they couldn't or didn't want to get with the program, despite the support we offered. Sometimes making fundamental changes to your behavior and applying them consistently is just too hard." The term "change strategy" triggers a flood of new questions in Smith, but she needs to make a stand-up meeting and doesn't want to be late. So she asks whether Davidson has time for another discussion. "Let's see," she says, "my schedule is full, but why don't you come by for lunch on Sunday, I've got all the time in the world for you then!"

On Thursday evening, Smith gets a call from Foster. "Is everything OK?" she asks, "It's great to hear from you!" "It's taking some getting used to, not just for me, but for everyone, but I think things are going pretty well." "How's Lean in Careville?" Smith follows up. "Eh, moving along slowly but surely in the ER, but everything else is pretty much at a standstill. I think everyone's waiting for you to get back. But actually, that's not why I called," he says hesitantly, "I had a major run-in with Cameron." "Go on," encourages Smith. Long story short, Morton demanded that Foster reinstate the age-old tradition of workplace meetings and that he had to "finally" submit the management report within 24 hours. "That's awful, how did you respond?" Foster explains that he—in line with Smith's approach—informed Morton that the daily stand-up meetings were far more productive than weekly meetings. He also invited Morton to attend a few, so he could witness it with his own eyes. But Morton was not to be swayed, so Foster really needed some good advice. Smith encourages him and explains that Morton is occasionally entirely impossible to deal with. She gives him a few tips and tells him not to hesitate to call her if he runs into any more problems. A little while later, Smith calls Torres to discuss matters. As she had expected, he was already aware of the incident with Morton. "You know, Jeanne, I'm getting sick and tired of that man," says Torres, "enough is enough. How are things in Oregon?" Smith enthusiastically shares her experiences, and Torres listens and responds ... the "short call" turns into a long and valuable discussion. (See Box 5.3)

BOX 5.3 EMOTIONAL INTELLIGENCE

A frequently used term in management literature is *emotional intelligence* (EI). Daniel Goleman (2012) was not the first, but is certainly the most cited author who claims that EI is a more important indicator for human success than cognitive intelligence, expressed as intelligence quotient. EI is, according to Wikipedia: "the ability to identify, assess, and control the emotions of oneself, of others, and of groups."

The ability to gauge which emotions are simmering below the surface, behind the spreadsheets—and addressing them with the right tone—can mean the difference between success and failure in terms of bringing people on board. This applies to almost every leadership situation, and certainly to Lean.

A good (Lean) leader must be able to asses where and most importantly why resistance develops. Resistance is not a bad thing, because it means people are involved. In fact, if there is no resistance to change, "you risk slipping," as a member of the Board of Directors of a large hospital once said. Gauging the value of resistance often requires more than just a rational approach.

Sensitivity to emotions is also important, as they can lead to suboptimal decisions. How to handle dissatisfaction with wait times among patients—and among doctors and nurses—in relation to staffing and budget constraints? For example, how do you shift attention from quantity (more manpower) to effectiveness and efficiency (working smarter with the same people), without making this seem like a lack of empathy. As a leader requires not only compassion, but also the ability to stay first: be tough, but with heart.

Emotions can also be used to support the burning platform, the critical need for change. Unfortunately, there are more than enough recent examples of bottlenecks in care institutions that made headlines. This creates a great deal of anger within the

(Continued)

BOX 5.3 (*CONTINUED*)   EMOTIONAL INTELLIGENCE

organization about how things were handled, and how it damages the reputation of the system as a whole. These types of (negative) emotions can be used as a powerful motivator for change and improvement. A great deal of EI is required to guide these precarious processes in the right direction. A volcano can provide a lot of positive energy, but there is always a risk of premature eruption.

Smith notices that a negative experience, like that night with the senior citizens with food poisoning, can provide an extra stimulus to get things moving. The way that a junior responds to resistance by Fernandez is also essential to the transformation process in her department. At the same time, she is unable to get a handle on Morton. The first experiences her interim replacement, Foster, has with him are also hardly encouraging.

During the feedback session with Karlsson on Friday afternoon, Smith talks about the discussion she had with Davidson. "Yeah, Margo is great," replies Karlsson, "When push comes to shove, she's always ready to invite you over for a Sunday lunch. I've been to a few, and it's always a pleasure—gastronomically as well, I might add." The discussion quickly turns to change management. Karlsson has a clear vision on the subject. "Keywords are start small, expand slowly, maximize incidents to underline the need for change, and above all: have a clear vision of the future along and sail a steady course, no matter the weather! Also," she continues, "unconditional and visible support from the top is essential. That was a problem here at first, but then Ingrid joined the Board, and publicly gave Lean her support. Actually, she did more than that. She personally attended all kinds of sessions, which was really special and generated a huge amount of goodwill for both her and Lean. I have noticed that Ingrid is always ready to roll up her sleeves and talk to people, and she's always respectful, but she does expect something in return.

For example, she noticed that a lot of employees were unfamiliar with procedures for a Code call. Until she got involved, it had proven impossible to get all the right people in the same room at the same time to address the problems. Pearson sat down with those responsible that very afternoon to find a solution and kept close tabs on the process to check for results. Watching that process was a unique experience. She clearly stated everyone had to be informed, but gave the team leaders room to work toward a solution themselves. Even when the initial attempts failed to provide the desired result, she continued to ask about the next step toward achieving the goal and most importantly about what they learned in the process. We eventually reached the goal, and everyone involved learned a great deal.

"We also noticed that change really is an active verb," Karlsson continues. "That means employees need to change from within, that you need to stimulate them, enable them to change. All too often, I've witnessed managers try to change their employees, often without lasting success. As soon as a manager looks the other way, people go back to business as usual." They decide Smith should take a close look at change aspects during her third week. Karlsson suspects there may be some change fatigue present and that a few new interventions may be needed.

That Sunday, Smith has lunch at Davidson's beautiful seaside home. After a delicious meal, they share a cup of tea and discuss change management further. Davidson explains how she supervised an ambitious student working on a thesis in change management a few years back. She had focused specifically on the introduction of Lean in the RKH and the role of leadership in that process. She recommends Smith look up the thesis. "That was

BOX 5.4   LEAN LEADERSHIP FROM A CHANGE MANAGEMENT PERSPECTIVE

Many publications on Lean make it clear that Lean is not a collection of tricks, but more of an art form, or rather, a management philosophy: an integrated, consistent approach based on deep conviction and insights. Not something that can be introduced on a weekday afternoon. Lean is a commitment and requires implementation at the mental, strategic, and operational level. Change management is essential to this process.

Hundreds of books have been written on change management. The color print concept by De Caluwé and Vermaak (2006), for example, is a part of the standard toolkit for many.

In this box, we briefly outline the development of change management and present a few current models. If you are *integrally* responsible for the implementation of Lean thinking and actions, we recommend you delve deeper into this key topic and seek out professional support as necessary.

CHANGE MANAGEMENT IS A BROAD TERM WITH A RICH HISTORY

Change management may draw from a variety of schools and disciplines, some of them interconnected (based on Mintzberg et al., 1998), such as:

- The Design school: change management as a conceptual process
- The Entrepreneurial school: change management as a visionary process
- The Learning school: change management as a creative process
- The Political school: change management as a power process
- The Cultural school: change management as an ideological process

These schools of thought and philosophies are the foundation for fulfilling the assignment set to managers and consultants by Drucker (1957), an assignment that also applies to Lean and is still relevant today: "Realizing goals by systematically and methodically doing what used to be done based on feeling and intuition, to distill what was once left to experience into principles and concepts, and replace empirical knowledge with a logical schematic that is internally consistent."

The Change Model by Ten Have

The PROMIIC model by Ten Have and others (2015) allows organizations to change effectively and professionally. PROMIIC stands for Process Model for Integral and Intentional Change. An effective change process is defined by the change force present within an organization: a powerful change vision and change capacity. Change strength, according to them, is based on five crucial factors: rationale, effect, focus, energy, and cohesion:

1. Rationale: the idea underlying a specific change, in logical and visionary terms. The rational represents the impetus for change and must not only be right but also be engaging.

(Continued)

**BOX 5.4 (*CONTINUED*)   LEAN LEADERSHIP FROM
A CHANGE MANAGEMENT PERSPECTIVE**

2. Effect: the desired, projected, or experienced concrete effect of the change on various involved parties (advantages or disadvantages, positive or negative results, perceptions and feelings).

3. Focus: the direction and indications as provided by or derived from the reference framework created by, among other things, organizational values, strategy, and structure.

4. Energy: the inspiration, motivation, and capacity that determine, for instance, leadership and the availability of knowledge and resources that will determine the feasibility of the change.

5. Cohesion: the guidance and coherence that ensure consistency and connection, and which—combined with the four other core elements—allow the efforts for change to perform optimally.

Based on these key success factors, Ten Have defined a "formula" for an organization's change force (Figure 5.2):

Change Force = (Rationale * Effect * Focus * Energy)^{Cohesion}

Change competence model

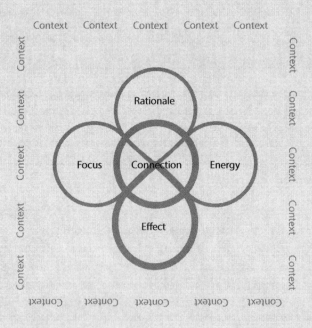

FIGURE 5.2
The elemental change model. (From Ten Have, S. et al., *Change Competence: Implementing Effective Change*, Routledge, New York, NY, 2015. With permission.)

(Continued)

BOX 5.4 (*CONTINUED*)   LEAN LEADERSHIP FROM A CHANGE MANAGEMENT PERSPECTIVE

Change Strategies

A well-known and oft-cited change philosophy is that of Bennis, Benne, and Chin (1979, 1985). They distinguish three main strategies:

1. *Force of power*, where a certain change is forced through from a position of power. This is a top-down approach. Power is necessary, is the assumption, to force the desired behavior.

2. *Rational-empirical*, in which it is assumed that employees are rational creatures who allow themselves to be led by rational self-interest.

3. *Normative reeducational*, aims to promote people toward changes via self-generated improvement proposals. This is a bottom-up strategy. The underlying view is that people are (also) active by nature, seek meaning, and are willing to learn.

The third strategy best fits Lean, while the first is the worst fit: employees shape change, while leaders are expected to provide direction and keep things on course and properly apply the methods.

In their model, Bennis, Benne, and Chin recognized the importance of, among other things, the planned nature of change processes, the use of interventions to influence the change process, and emphasis on behavioral change.

Boonstra (1992) adds a fourth strategy, the so-called barter reward: people make their own cost–benefit analysis and determine what the change will provide. Later, he (Boonstra, 2000) added chaos theory as a fifth strategy, based on the principle that activities, processes, and involved employees organize themselves to whatever degree is necessary (Table 5.1).

This overview by Boonstra is consistent with that of De Caluwé and Vermaak (2006). They also distinguish five approaches to change, based on the dominant cultural characteristics and customs within organizations (Table 5.2). These determine which "color print(s)" and associated interventions are expected to be most effective.

TABLE 5.1

Change Strategies

Power strategy	Planned strategy	Negotiation strategy	Programmatic strategy	Interactive strategy
Pushing through	Moving	Negotiating	Pulling	Exploring
Top-down	Initiative lies with	More parties	Participatory	Interactive
Goal oriented	the top	Result oriented	Problem oriented	Future oriented
Legitimate power	Goal oriented	Positional Power	Indirect power	Imagination
Controller input	Expert power	Party input	Employee input	Working together
Power coercion	Expert	Negotiation	Normative-	Dialog and conflict
No participation	contributions	Political process	reeducational	A lot of interaction
	Rational-empirical		A lot of	
	Little participation		participation	
Cynical	Skeptical	Political	Yearning	Innovative

Source: Data from Boonstra, J.J., Leren Veranderen, *M&O, tijdschrift voor management en organisatie,* 54(1), 81–6, 2000.

(*Continued*)

BOX 5.4 (*CONTINUED*)   LEAN LEADERSHIP FROM A CHANGE MANAGEMENT PERSPECTIVE

TABLE 5.2

Five Approach to Change

Color	Nothing Changes If You ...	In a ...	Into a ...
Yellow	Bring interests together	Power play	A viable solution, win-win
Blue	First think and then (planned) do	Rational process	The best solution
Red	Stimulate people the right way	Barter exercise	A motivating solution, the best fit
Green	Put people in learning situations	Learning process	A solution that people find together
White	Leaves room for spontaneous evolution	Dynamic process	A solution that releases energy

Source: Data from De Caluwé, L. and Vermaak, H., *Leren Veranderen: Een Handboek Voor De Veranderkundige,* Kluwer, Deventer, 2006.

Kotter

According to Kotter (1997, 1999), leadership is about constructive or adaptive change. A leader creates a vision and provides strategic direction. He tries to inspire and motivate employees through communication, and get everyone facing the same direction. Along with many others, Kotter believes that management and leadership are very different and (can) complement each other. See Box 3.2 for more on these differences. In a stable, controllable transition, Kotter believes leadership is less important than management. However, change is the anathema of stability.

According to Kotter, the problem lies with the rate of change, which tends to be very high these days, greatly increasing the need for leadership. Kotter distinguishes several sequential steps to introduce change in organizations (see Box 2.3). His vision on leadership is crystal clear and extremely relevant to Lean. Regarding good leadership, he states that leaders:

1. Help people build a vision of a future that is better than the present and provide a strategy to reach it.
2. Subsequently communicate this vision and strategy to as many people as possible to make sure people not only understand but also see that it is extremely logical.
3. Create a motivating environment.
4. Demonstrate "executive temperament"—be tough when necessary and steadfast in the face of adversity.
5. Be self-aware: able to balance work life and private life, aware of personal limits and blind spots.

Individuals, no matter how influential or charismatic, never have within themselves all the properties required to overcome reluctance and tradition, except in very small organizations. Kotter points out that short-term gains are sometimes possible, though success is often short lived in the absence of a strong guiding coalition. This not only

(*Continued*)

BOX 5.4 (*CONTINUED*)   LEAN LEADERSHIP FROM A CHANGE MANAGEMENT PERSPECTIVE

refers to the head of an organization, but also to a group of five or more people who surround him and must commit to better performance. Even if satisfaction with the current situation is relatively poor, organizations often underestimate the need for such a team; they assume that changes can be led by an appointed team of executors or by a quality or change department. The importance of such a guiding coalition is also visible at Careville UMC. In addition to Patterson at the top level, Torres, Smith, Foster and—gradually—Fernandez and McLaughlin are all members.

In Closing

Change is a complex process due to the multitude of factors that play a role. Many complex change processes ultimately fail to provide the desired result. The literature provides a variety of step-by-step plans, conditions, and success factors for change. However, such step-by-step plans and summaries are never complete.

Other factors may always play a part. Step-by-step plans are also self-fulfilling prophecies, as they are relatively impervious to reality. Reality is usually a little rough around the edges, exciting and unpredictable. You should take a multitude of (f)actors into account when selecting a model for change.

Successful change strategies often succeed due to the following:

- A focus on concrete operational problems
- Making employees who face these problems responsible for solving them
- Consistently implementing collective learning processes on a small scale

An effective way to change behavior is to place employees and managers in new strategic *settings*, with new roles and responsibilities. For example by assigning a single nurse to each patient, instead of having all nurses be responsible for all patients at once. This can create a context that "forces" people into a new attitude and new behaviors. An improvement culture that helps employees directly link the improvements achieved and their own input can also develop, which is an essential part of Lean philosophy.

Smith noticed that the RKH consciously thinks and acts in terms of change management, and that there is an understanding the a new "picture" and new interventions are continuously needed. The discussion with Davidson underlines this.

some excellent research," says Davidson. "The philosophies of Kotter as well as those of other Dutch authors, such as Ten Have and his Process Model for Integral and Intentional Change (PROMIIC) model, and the color print concept by De Caluwé and Vermaak, helped a great deal. (See Box 5.4) Particularly because it is important to be able to fall back onto a wide range of tools to suit the situation. If all you have is a hammer, everything is a nail!"

Back at her own temporary abode later that afternoon, Smith tries to make sense of it all. Despite—or perhaps thanks to—the excellent wine Davidson served with lunch, a picture is starting to form of the "character traits of a Lean leader." Listening, coaching, nondirective, involved, and steadfast quickly make the list. She e-mails Karlsson and asks her to contribute. Karlsson replies immediately, intrigued by the idea of creating a platonic ideal of a Lean leader. In her e-mail, she promises to introduce Smith to their HR director, who she thinks will have some interesting views on the subject. Particularly because he was closely involved in the exit interviews with departing managers, so he's in a unique position to provide non-examples. Smith then jots down a few more thoughts on change management; that was the excuse for the extended lunch with Davidson, after all. The color print concept appeals to her, and she jots down greenprint and blueprint as the key approaches they implemented here. Later that evening, Smith has a long Skype chat with her husband. She talks to him about Lean leaders as well, and together they come up with a few more interesting additions—"humility" and "leadership by example" are perhaps the most noteworthy. "Yeah," says Tom, "a tough character trait is also needed, something like 'steadfastness' or 'courage to intervene'."

Week Three

Karlsson is true to her word and takes Smith to meet Jacob Vargas, HR director the following Monday. They make an appointment to talk, and Vargas promises to give some thought to the characteristics of a Lean leader. Before she leaves, he asks Smith: "What about you, do you have a clear picture yet? Why don't you e-mail it me, it should help me hone my thoughts." Yet another leader, and not a manager, Smith thinks to herself. Smith spends the rest of the day in an improvement session in the ER and notices that a lot of the improvements appear to be small. At the same time, she realizes that these small improvements are clear steps in the direction the ER wants to head. She also quickly identifies a bottleneck that isn't immediately obvious during the improvement sessions: she talks to a new employee who has only just started working at the RKH. One of his colleagues told him he needed to clear his action list in the procurement system, which was overflowing. "Oh," replied the newcomer, "I didn't even know I had an action list, where can I find it?" Smith suggests taking a closer look at the procedure for training new employees, to prevent this type of thing from happening again.

At the end of the day, the department head Eric Taylor invites her out to dinner in town. Smith is up for an evening out on the town, and after a good meal, they dig into one of Smith's favorite subjects: the relationship between Lean and leadership. The discussion with Foster about Morton's management style fresh on her mind, she asks Taylor: "Eric, I assume you also have a few managers who prefer to manage than lead." Taylor nods, and Smith continues: "How do you deal with that?" "If they really don't want to change: ignore them," is his initial response. Smith isn't satisfied with the answer: "Yeah, I do that sometimes, but you have to find a way to create a decent working relationship." Taylor ponders this for a while, nods, and replies: "Because they're a minority here, and because the top of the organization has a very strong focus on servant leadership, those old-fashioned managers have it tough. Some of them have adapted, others just left. Our Board of Directors is pretty strict on that point, Ingrid is particularly tough on the "alpha male" behavior." "OK," says Smith, "and do you have any idea what criteria they use for selecting replacements?" Taylor realizes he doesn't really know. "That's an interesting question Jeanne," he says, "and I'm going to try and find the answer. I'll put it in my report."

Early the next morning, Smith talks to Vargas. She takes an immediate liking to him, for his style more than his dark curls: he takes her along into the workplace and regularly talks to a manager. A number of brief three-way meetings quickly makes it clear that Vargas is not directive at all, but is respected wherever he goes. The man exudes calm and spends very little time actually talking, preferring to let the other say his piece. By asking smart questions about what the manager is working on, what he hopes to achieve, and what he has learned from the steps taken in the process, he retrieves a wealth of information, and an hour later, Smith is beginning to understand how Vargas manages it. By asking people what they have learned—even from actions that didn't yield the desired result—he stimulates people to act and think about what went well, and what went less well. This gives them better insight into the processes within the organization and how they can improve them. After the intensive tour of the clinic, they have a cup of coffee in his office—the door of which is always open. "Well, Jeanne, what do you think? Particularly relating to your previous considerations. I read your e-mail, and I think you were right on all counts." Smith ponders: "I'm particularly impressed with how you approach people, Jacob. You say very little, but get a lot from them." "Is that so?" he asks. "I paid attention during two of the meetings, and you talked for less than 10% of the time in each," she replied. "Interesting idea, keeping track," he replies, "what made you think to do that?" Their conversation continues and toward the end of the meeting she makes another appointment near the end of her internship, because Vargas is very interested in finding out about her profile of a Lean leader. "Isn't that something you've got sorted out already?" Smith asks him. He somewhat cryptically responds that that is not the interesting question.

Smith spends the rest of the week working hard at the hospital during the day, and devouring the *Toyota Kata* in the evenings. She also calls her former colleague Rachel Jameson, who she assumes has also read the book. Jameson is glad to hear from her, but confesses she couldn't get through that particular tome. "It's not an easy read, is it," she says. Smith agrees the book certainly isn't a great work of literature, but she finds the subject matter so interesting she has to force herself to put it aside before bed. "OK," says Jameson, "so give me one key point you've gleaned from it." "Where to start?" replies Smith. "Know where you want to go, know where you are now, and make sure you take small steps towards improvement, while making sure you're moving towards your goal. And be certain to learn from the things you've done. In short, shoot straight and true, don't use buckshot."

After that, she places a Skype call to her husband and tells him about her unique experience with Vargas. "The man is a genius when it comes to asking effective questions. No clue if he's any good as an HR director, but considering how many great leaders are walking around here, I assume his contribution was significant," she says. "What about the doctors in the Robert Kennedy?" her husband asks. "Do you see any leadership qualities there, or are they uninterested in that?" Smith had already talked to a number of doctors and says: "That's been a very pleasant surprise, they're also extremely cooperative. Much more so than I'm used to back home. But they're also strong and self-assured, there's no shyness there. You know, Tom, that's a good question for Jacob Vargas."

On Friday, Torres calls Smith to discuss the upcoming workplace visit. "Patterson's coming, of course," he starts, "and I wasn't able to stop Morton from tagging along, and Fernandez had some excuse for not being able to make it. Ellen Kowalski is also coming along, and I think Jonathan should also be part of the team—what do you think?" he asks Smith. "Sounds good to me," she replies. "I assume you're also coming, right Luis?" she asks, making sure. Smith continues: "I suggest two themes—Lean and leadership." Torres is enthusiastic, and they go over a few more details, and then it is time for Smith to head to a meeting. As usual, they finish the week with a feedback session with Karlsson. Smith brings up the subject of leadership among the doctors. "Is that something you look at specifically?" she asks Karlsson. "Yes, it is. It's an important aspect when it comes to appointing department heads, and we organize master classes to help them make the shift from management to leadership. But we don't get rid of the crucial planning and control principles of management." "And it's working," replies Smith, "I'm really impressed!" "Well," says Karlsson, "I think a lot of it is about setting the right example."

Smith's final weekend in Oregon is a real pleasure. On Saturday, she heads to Portland with a few colleagues, and the Sunday is spent sailing with Karlsson, followed by a wonderful dinner at her seaside home. Of course, dinner talk quickly turns to work. Smith shares a few experiences from Careville and Karlsson asks her what she can expect from Morton. "Well," replies Smith, "he looks pretty harmless in his shirt and corduroy jacket. But if he doesn't like how things are going, he can get extremely contrary." "And what does that mean, exactly?" Karlsson wants to know. "It's always the same old tune," replies Smith, "he puts his foot down, insists on a specific report or form, without explaining why that's actually necessary. He's all about the rules, coaching doesn't really enter into it. Very different from what I see here." "Doesn't anybody coach you at Careville?" Karlsson asks, concerned. "Luckily there is, Luis Torres is fantastic, and Bob Patterson is slowly growing into the role," replies Smith. "I can't wait to meet them all," says Karlsson.

The Final Week

To make sure she gets all the details, Smith talks to a variety of team leaders about the way doctors lead them. The efforts to instill "servant" leadership in the doctors is bearing fruit: most team leaders have little difficulty describing the changes that have been made over the past 2 to 3 years, and all of them are pleased with the developments. The atmosphere is more open, and there's more dialog, they conclude. "We have less trouble with big egos, they deal with that better. That's mostly thanks to the stand-up sessions: lines are much shorter. We spend more time talking about the patients, which is what it's all about," says one of the team leaders. "For example, forms were often not completed, and patients regularly ended up with the wrong appointment because the administrative staff didn't have the information they needed. That's a rarity now."

She also asks one of the doctors, who replies: "Yeah, we were often stuck in old management paradigms, we thought we needed to manage based on output and prescriptions. Now we focus on the process and more stimulation, and we've noticed we get a lot more out of the teams." Then Smith asks what the doctor thinks about Lean, to which she responds: "I was extremely skeptical for a long time, but once my colleagues in internal medicine started showing results, both small and large, I got on board. Now I'm completely convinced it's useful, care is improving a little bit each day." "Do you also attend the stand-up sessions?" Smith asks. "I do my best, but I only really make it once a week. I do recommend it to everyone, though. You know, there's a session tomorrow morning that I'm attending, why don't you attend?" Smith immediately decides she should stimulate her colleague McLaughlin to participate more actively in the Lean sessions; he is not really involved in practice, she realizes. It is too bad he is not here to see how it affects people with his own eyes.

The next day, Smith attends the stand-up session and witnesses firsthand how the pulmonologist supports it energetically with her active, coaching approach. After the stand-up session, Smith participates in one more ER improvement session. Eric Taylor had to take his daughter to the general practitioner unexpectedly and asked her to lead the session in his place. After the session, she briefly asks the team to discuss how they think it went. The team is happy with her performance—a different style to Taylor, but none the worse for it. Taylor is back at work by then, and she briefly updates him on what happened and the results they achieved. "Great," he says, "I'm going to miss having you around next week!" Smith spends the rest of the day working on a first draft of her internship report. The section on Lean is fairly straightforward, she has a clear idea of the plan she wants to propose. She's collected so many impressions of leadership, however, that she's feeling an urgent need for a structure she can use to connect the various styles and theories with each other in a logical way. She discusses the issue with her husband that evening, who spontaneously starts drawing puzzle pieces. "That might just work," says Smith, "I'll sleep on it."

On Wednesday, Smith makes final arrangements for the arrival of the delegation from Careville together with Karlsson. She also attends a few sessions and continues working on her report. Toward the end of the workday, she spends an hour talking to Jacob Vargas about leadership and discusses her model-in-progress of puzzle pieces. He likes the idea and makes a number of valuable suggestions. Smith heads home energized and continues working on her report all evening. (See Box 5.5)

BOX 5.5   LEAN LEADERSHIP AT TOYOTA

A quest for the secrets of Lean leadership is impossible without the insights of Liker and Convis (2012) and Spear (2004). They emphasize that leadership entails coaching which focuses on personal and employee development. This development should take place close to the workplace, by testing and implementing small changes on a daily basis. Human and organizational development go hand in hand as part of a coordinated process.

Liker and Convis compared leadership at Toyota with traditional leadership. They conclude that where traditional leadership focuses on the individual, leadership at Toyota—in addition to being focused on the individual—is explicitly also institutional: from the Chief Executive Officer to the team leader. At every hierarchical level, people are expected to work on their own development, improve their skills and lead in a way that creates consensus and promotes development. A Toyota leader has a strong personality and is capable of providing his team with clear direction. He also has a sharp eye for his people's development. To this end, he tries to understand the primary process in detail. The Toyota leader does not stay in his office, but is often found in the workplace. This is in stark contrast to leaders who define the big picture from a distance.

Liker and Convis present four levels of Lean leadership at Toyota (Table 5.3).

TABLE 5.3

Four levels of Lean Leadership at Toyota

Level 1: Self-Development		
Skill	Leadership quality and potential	Looks for possibilities for improvement and aligns them with the values of Toyota
Process	Learning and growth	Goes to the shop floor to fully understand the situation and problems faced. Works toward increasingly challenging goals based on this knowledge, supported by a mentor.
Level 2: Coaching and Developing Others		
Skill	Developing the next generation of leaders	Learns to see strength and areas for development in others, how to create a growth-promoting situation, and how to optimize the impact of coaching by minimizing interventions during coaching moments. Develops individuals in the desired direction and closely monitors the results.
Process	Coaching and development of others	Takes responsibility for proactively helping people in the self-development learning cycle.
Level 3: Supporting Kaizen (Continuous Improvement)		
Skill	Achieving goals	Learns how to develop leadership at various levels within the organization using standards, goals, and visual management.

(Continued)

BOX 5.5 *(CONTINUED)*   LEAN LEADERSHIP AT TOYOTA

Process	Enable process improvements	Is present on the shop floor in order to identify deviations from goals through visual management. Coaches others to take their responsibility for restoring these deviations.

Level 4: Creating Vision and Align Goals to This Vision

Skill	Developing a vision and plan	Creates support for the goals and organizes a participatory process in order to translate this to subgoals.
Process	Set goals, align associated plans with vision.	Initiates and maintains continuous improvement by guiding toward (sub-)goals using visual management. Focuses on solving problems and developing individuals.

Source: Data from Liker, J.K. and Convis, G.L. *The Toyota Way to Lean Leadership. Achieving and Sustaining Excellence Through Leadership Development*, McGraw-Hill, New York, 2012.

A talented leader at Toyota is coached in the development of his skills on each of the levels listed above, during his entire career. All levels are addressed at each stage of his career, though the emphasis shifts over time. As experience is gained, and a person develops more experience and faces greater challenges, focus will shift to level 4; however, level 1 is never considered complete.

Additionally, whether development is aligned with the core values of the (Toyota) organization is monitored at every level: *spirit of challenge*, continuous drive for improvement, visiting the shop floor, teamwork, and respect for people.

You can read more about developing people in Boxes 5.2 and 6.1.

A Delegation from Careville

The delegation from Careville took a red-eye out to Portland and arrives at the RKH at 10 AM. To Smith's surprise, Peter Jacobs has also come along, the cardiologist who previously strongly rejected the request for participation. "What's he doing here?" she asks Torres the first chance she gets. "It turns out a former college buddy works here, and he cleared his schedule last minute to make sure he could tag along," replies Torres. "Oh, and Ellen Kowalski canceled last minute, by the way," he adds. After a cup of coffee and a brief tour, it is time for an official welcome by Ingrid Pearson. Smith notes how warmly Pearson and Patterson greet each other. After the required niceties have been observed, Patterson explains his plans for Careville, and that they're extremely eager to take a look behind the scenes at the RKH. "That's all well and good," replies Pearson, "but I've got a question for you too: we're doing well with Lean, if I do say so myself, but we're also ready to take the next step. In short, please pay close attention, ask any questions you want, and I look forward to hearing your suggestions tomorrow afternoon." "We gladly accept the challenge, Ingrid," says Patterson.

"First, I want to show you our pride and joy," continues Pearson and takes them along to the Cardiology ward. "The nursing ward was recently remodeled," she explains and shows them a fully updated system for bandages, medication, and other materials. The nurses no longer need to walk back and forth between patients and the supply closets in the hall, but have direct access to everything they need in a cabinet by the bedside. The cabinet are stocked from the hallway by the pharmacy, and the nurses take what they need in the rooms. "That was a complicated puzzle to solve," says Pearson, "and it took us quite a bit of time to sort out the value stream with the Pharmacy, but we're extremely pleased with how it's going." They then split into pairs and visit a variety of different teams to experience how Lean works here in the Pacific Northwest.

That evening, most of the Careville delegation has dinner with Karlsson and Davidson. Patterson is out with Pearson, and Jacobs is catching up with his college buddy. Over dinner, Torres and Foster go back and forth, talking about what they have seen and experienced. They're impressed, particularly by the fact Lean appears to have taken roots at the heart of the organization. Davidson and Karlsson explain the road getting there was long, but they are extremely proud of their achievements. Then Morton asks what Lean actually cost them to date. "About $1 million a year, I'd guess," says Davidson. "And you've been doing that for four years, so $5 million to date," replies Morton, "and what about gains?" Smith sees Torres' face go blank, but he keeps quiet. "Actually," replies Karlsson, "we never really measured that. What we do know …" she continues, but is interrupted by Morton, who says: "So you've spent $5 million, and you have no idea what it's gotten you? We're not going to do that!" Torres grasps the opportunity and asks Karlsson what she was saying before being interrupted. "Look," she says, "of course $5 million is a lot of money, but if you look at the improvements in the quality of care we provide, I think it was worth every penny. We have shorter wait times at the outpatient clinic, fewer cancelled operations, and above all, the number of incidents has decreased significantly. And I can also proudly state that absenteeism has dropped from over 6% to a mere 4.5%." Morton keeps hacking away, until Torres whispers to him: "Cameron, lay off, we're guests here, remember?"

The dinner is over soon after this embarrassing interlude. Torres apologizes to Davidson and Karlsson, who tell him: "That's precisely the kind of attitude you don't want for Lean. We used to have his type here as well, but almost all of them have left by now. I think you need to get rid of this guy as quickly as possible," says Davidson quietly. Karlsson decides to take the bull by the horns. When they're parting ways, she takes Morton by the shoulder, and asks: "Cameron, what is it you're so scared of?"

During breakfast at the hotel, the delegation is complete, joined by Smith. Patterson is in high spirits. Jacobs is talking a mile a minute and exclaims his college buddy told him a few things about Lean that he found "pretty interesting." "Give me an example," Smith asks him. With a glint in his eye, he talks about how they end each day here with a half-hour meeting between doctors and nurses on the ward. "And you know the best thing," he says, "it prevents half of the calls the doctors get at night!" They finish up and head to the hospital for another day's work. Smith goes to the ER with Foster and introduces him to Eric Taylor and his team. Foster takes a good look around and then attends the final Lean session of the week on the ER. Smith finds Torres and talks about Lean leadership with him and Vargas. Torres wants to figure out how the RKH managed to ensure a majority of the "old-fashioned" managers developed into modern leaders. "Well," says Vargas, "we did our best to promote turnover, but most importantly, we invested heavily in the change process: we created an intensive coaching program. And we reaped the benefits, particularly among medical staff. We've noticed that respect and mutual understanding are now the foundation of cooperation, which makes resolving bottlenecks between various departments much easier."

"How did you tackle that, Jacob?" asks Smith. Vargas briefly outlines the path they followed, underlining that in his view, leadership by example from the Board of Directors was and remains essential to this process. "We regularly reflect with the Board to make sure we are still on course." "Who is 'we', exactly?" asks Torres. The "we" in question includes the HR director, the Strategy and Policy director and the entire Board of Directors. Finally, Vargas adds: "Remember, we've been tugging at them for four years now, and it hasn't all been smooth sailing. It's not always easy—old behaviors still rear their ugly head from time to time, and it's tough to get rid of them."

There's a final meeting at the end of the afternoon. "Well, what did you think?" Pearson asks her guests. Patterson subtly gestures to Smith, indicating she should take the lead. Smith enthusiastically talks about how much she learned and how fantastic it was to be granted a look behind the scenes. "And what's your advice for us?" asks Karlsson. Smith clearly outlines a number of options the RKH could select from. "The way I see things," she begins, "you still have a lot to gain by paying closer attention to the value streams *between* departments. And I think your department heads and division managers will face quite a few challenges tackling those bottlenecks. It's the same issue we run into at Careville: when push comes to shove, the interests of the department often appear to outweigh those of the patient, which is unacceptable, of course." Pearson is impressed. "And you noticed that in just four weeks," she comments. Torres is next to speak. He is a little envious of how the RKH has managed to make a giant leap and put leadership at the forefront. Then it is Foster's turn, but Morton interrupts. "Actually," he says, "I'm perplexed. You spend millions on Lean, and I can't really see where you plan on earning that back. All I see is more work, all those stand-up meetings and improvement sessions and so on, that keeps people from doing their jobs. What's wrong with good, strict management reporting?" Pearson asks him: "What were you expecting, Cameron?" "Um," he stammers, "I thought Lean was some sort of goose that laid the golden eggs, and that you would show us a presentation outlining all of the savings." "So why do you think we didn't do it?" asks Pearson. "Erm, I assume because there is not profit?" Pearson gives Karlsson a signal, who turns on the projector. "Look," says Karlsson, "these are our profits over the past three years. The first slide shows how average patient satisfaction has increased from 6.3 to 7.6 over the past three years. This slide shows a reduction of 20% in the number of incidents per year. This next slide shows absenteeism numbers for medical and supporting staff, which have also decreased substantially. Anything else you'd like to know?" Pearson asks. Morton is turning bright red and is sinking into his chair.

They end the visit informally with dinner that evening. Morton has decided not to attend and it turns into a great evening. Toward the end, people trickle out, and only Patterson and Pearson are left. The next morning, Morton is the first one down to breakfast, as if nothing had happened. Patterson doesn't show, letting them know by text message that he'll meet them at the airport. On the flight back, Smith ponders her Oregon experience, but soon dozes off.

Patterson managed to convince Karlsson to help her shape the Lean process at Careville for the next 3 years .... This allows them to reach every nook and cranny in the hospital with unprecedented speed and achieve fantastic results .... Coaching is the new normal for managers, and management reports are designed to serve patient interests .... Even curmudgeonly Cameron Morton has succumbed to Lean, finally accepting that operations should be focused on optimal treatment for the patient .... When Smith follows another patient who comes in with a broken arm, she is back at her desk within an hour, and the patient is already on the way home ....

Smith is jolted awake when the wheels touch down a few hours later. Her husband picks her up, and they spend the weekend catching up.

Reflection

In Oregon, Smith sees how Lean can change a large hospital for the better. Lean was not introduced "separately" in the RKH, but as part of a major push toward modernizing management: the shift from "traditional management" to Lean leadership was initiated and very successful. A coaching attitude from leaders is essential to success. It is a leader's task to develop the employee and increase his problem-solving capacity—something that must be done in the workplace, not from afar (we refer to this intensive form as close coaching). It is important to keep sight of the fact Lean is about changing the system, not dealing with individual behavior. Smith has witnessed how many people have discovered continuous improvement is not only efficient, but also fun.

Smith knows it's difficult to outline goals in a master plan and then move on to implementing such a plan. In the RKH, Smith discovers they have a plan that clearly states *what* they want to achieve: a description of the target situation. The next step is to embark on a journey toward that situation, deciding on which topic to address next at every new step along the way.

At the same time, Smith discovers there's still a lot to be done, which paradoxically is primarily due to improvements to interdepartmental processes. Apparently, the introduction of Lean leadership alone is not enough to do away with silo mentality. Smith correctly states that the patient, not the department, is of primary importance. Smith also discovers how crucial the Board of Directors and department heads are to a culture shift such as Lean. Even though the RKH is miles ahead of many other hospitals, humility and steadfastness are still present at all layers within the organization; learning is a continuous process, and nothing is ever good enough.

Change management insights and interventions are also required to ensure a fundamental transformation such as Lean takes root in an organization—creating a Lean organization requires all resistance to change to be surmounted or at least redirected. A solid approach based on a clear change strategy is essential.

In closing: Smith is given the opportunity to look behind the "Lean scenes" at another hospital. She already had a brief visit at the Asklepios Hospital. She realizes this has a powerful effect on her own knowledge and views on Lean. These inspiring workplace visits also show she is ready to learn and take the time to do so.

Lean Leadership Attributes

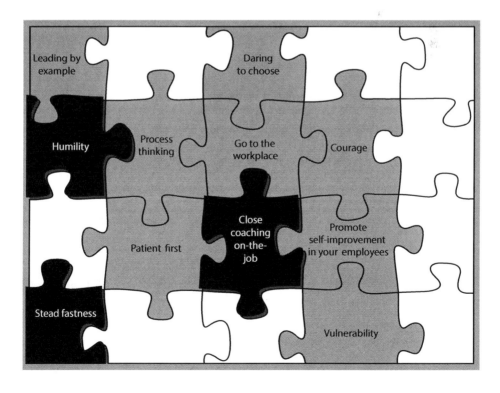

6

Beyond the Emergency Room

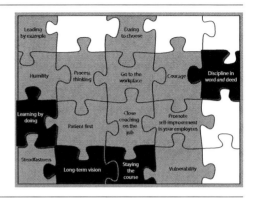

Case Study

After a fantastic, educational month in Oregon, Jeanne Smith returns home to Careville. During her stay in Oregon, Lean development has been on a slow burner at Careville. Now that Smith's back, she and her team pick up where they left off and forge ahead. The experiences from Oregon are a great help. Additionally, trust and belief in Lean among top management at Careville has been strengthened by the visit to the Robert Kennedy Hospital, which is a great help. The Lean program, scheduled to launch in a few months, is also under active development.

The First Day at Work

On Monday morning, Smith arrives at the hospital and goes straight to the emergency room (ER); after a few weeks in Oregon, it feels like coming home. Smith logs in and glances at her inbox; she kept on top of her e-mail while she was in Oregon, and the weekend was pretty quiet. Before she heads to her first appointment with Torres and Patterson, Foster shows up for the ER handover. Smith asks Foster how things are going: "How did you like running the ER for the past month?" "Not bad, took a bit of getting used to, but I had fun," he replies. "But I don't mind handing over the reins again, because it was tough. So, Jeanne, now that you've slept on it, what key conclusions did you take along from Oregon?" asks Foster. "I've got three main points," says Smith, "first, coaching is more important than management, and should be focused on development, not correction. Second, Lean isn't about tools, but about changing company culture. And third, if you're trying to improve things, start with a goal, and make changes if things don't work out, but keep that goal in sight." "That's a nice list," says Foster, "as long as we remember we need to keep moving toward the goals we've set." "But enough of that, let's get to work. I've got an appointment with Patterson to get to," Smith says, ending the discussion.

As Smith arrives at Patterson's office, Cameron Morton is just leaving. He looks despondent. "Good morning, Cameron!" she says, but he does not seem to see her. Once she is settled in Patterson's office, he says: "It's still confidential, but I thought you should know I asked Morton to vacate his position. The man has no feel for the new developments we're trying to introduce, and even when I try to explain how we want to do things and why, he reverts to his controlling behavior. He drove me crazy last week in Oregon, and things weren't any better this morning." Smith replies: "That's clear to me, I understand your decision and think it's for the best. I do regret not bringing up the negative influence Cameron was having earlier and more clearly," she adds.

Then Torres arrives and they discuss the Lean program and everything that needs to happen to get things ready to launch in 6 months. At the end of the meeting, Torres says: "Since we need to find a new Operations manager, how about making a serious attempt at defining a Lean leader profile? Jeanne was already working on that in Oregon, so I think it's something we can manage." Smith is on board with the idea and suggests talking it over with Human Resource (HR) department.

Smith spends the rest of the day getting back up to speed in the ER. That afternoon, she has a good talk with Ellen Kowalski, who immediately apologizes for her absence in Oregon. "There was a big fight happening between two department heads, so I thought leaving for two days would be unwise," she explains. "It was a good thing I was here, because I really had to get involved." "So, is everything under control again?" asks Smith. "Well," says Kowalski, "I doubt those two will ever become fast friends, but I think we found a way for them to work together professionally. Because I really don't feel like firing either of them." Smith also meets with McLaughlin and enthusiastically tells him about her experiences in Oregon. "So the doctors there are also actively involved with Lean?" asks McLaughlin. "That's right," says Smith, "it's really too bad you couldn't make the trip, you could have seen how important it is to them for yourself." "If I'm understanding you correctly, you think I should also be taking part in the stand-up meetings," replies McLaughlin. Smith confirms that and sees McLaughlin shift gears. "No problem," he says, "I'll try to make room in my schedule."

Moving Ahead with Lean

One of the things Smith learned in Oregon is that she needs to actively make room in her schedule for Lean. She blocks the first hour of each day for stand-up meetings and decides to schedule a daily start-up meeting with all of the team leaders, a meeting during which the expected bottlenecks of the day are addressed. She also blocks half an hour each afternoon to make sure that she's present at the shift change. Finally, she decides to check with the workplace whether the agreements they make are actually being followed.

During the course of the week, Smith talks to a number of department heads interested in getting started with Lean. Keeping the previous shortlist they drew up in the ER in mind, she tries to prioritize. She also speaks to Jessica Kern, from the HR department, about the desire to create a Lean leader profile. To Smith's surprise, Kern has been reading quite a bit about Lean and even visited the bank where her sister works to gain some insights in the HR aspects of Lean. Kern is enthusiastic about how that bank already adjusted most job descriptions to serve Lean goals. "What kind of changes were those?" asks Smith. Kern replied: "Two main aspects were key: first, the shift from managing to coaching, moving from controlling to personal responsibility. Second, a willingness to learn was included as a key skill. That's reflected by the job descriptions for management positions in particular, but that makes sense." This is consistent with Smith's ideas on the matter, and toward the end of the meeting, the profile begins to take shape. A key addition they come up with together is focused on creating a vision and, even more importantly, a path toward it. That evening, Smith jots down the changes they made that day and sends the profile to Jacob Vargas. She receives an almost immediate reply, stating that he would be happy to contribute and will get back to her later in the week.

The rest of the week flies past. Smith has her hands full defining the true north for the ER and is determined to flesh out the topic as quickly as possible. In Oregon, she discovered the importance of not trying to figure things out alone, but to work on a solution together with other actors in the department. Smith schedules a few meetings to address the issue.

In the meantime, it is becoming clear there are more than enough departments interested in participating in Lean. Despite this, Smith still believes the Board of Directors needs to take a more active role in the Lean program that's in the works. She discusses the issue with Torres, who supports her. They quickly agree it would be a good idea for Patterson and both of his colleagues to participate in a number of Lean sessions in the workplace. "That will shake things up," he says, "for themselves and the people in the workplace—they never see the Board." Torres agrees to raise the issue with the Board, and Smith knows it is in good hands: Torres always delivers on his promises.

The Lean Team

Smith also picks up where she left off with Townsend and Quinn, who are still hard at work implementing Lean in the ER. Smith has visited the workplace a few times already and participated in three stand-up meetings, and has the impression things are going well. She asks Townsend and Quinn what they think. "The fact that we can't start working with Cardiology is really becoming an issue," says Townsend. "Well, I have some good news for you then," says Smith, explaining how Jacobs "saw the light" in Oregon. "I'll see him on Monday, and my feeling is we'll be able to move forward quickly after that." "What about the pharmacy?" asks Quinn. Smith already talked to Frank Johnson, but that door hasn't been opened yet. "I'm still pondering my next step," she replies, "and I think I'm going to need Patterson for that.

But moving along," continues Smith, "how do you two feel about Lean, are you still enjoying it?" "Actually," says Townsend, "we work very well together, and we'd love to join in the big Lean program you'll be heading up soon." "Yeah, I'd love that too, and you're going to need a team," adds Quinn. "How do you see that working, exactly?" asks Smith, who realizes Quinn's contract has already been extended once and is almost ending. "Well," replies Quinn hesitantly, "I don't know if there's room for me, but I'd really love to move to the Lean program, and start working here full-time." Townsend says she would like to trade in her position as staff advisor for a full-time role as a Lean advisor. "Great, I was hoping you'd say that," Smith responds. "I'll get right on that. I can't make any promises, but I'll do my best!"

Lean Leaders

On Thursday evening, Smith gets a call from Morton. She is surprised; he has never called her at home before. He is unusually humble and asks Smith how she feels about the fact that he's been asked to vacate his post. "Look, Cameron," says Smith, "I've experienced firsthand how you tried to get a grip on my department via reports and other management principles. Maybe that's how things used to work, but Careville is changing quickly, and Lean means a different way of working. That means we need managers who can change, and that's something you haven't shown me you can do yet." "Really," responds Morton, "can you give me an example, because I'm really trying!" "So you don't recognize yourself in my description?" asks Smith. Morton responds: "Well, my behavior in Oregon last week probably wasn't ideal." Smith waits, silent. "What do you think I should do, Jeanne?" asks Morton. "That's not something I can decide for you, Cameron," replies Smith, "but you have to understand Careville is going through rapid change, and that's something you need to want to keep up with." "Right, thanks for your time," says Morton.

The next morning, Torres walks in and informs her Morton has tendered his resignation. At his own request, Patterson relieved him of all of his responsibilities and authority starting immediately. "That's the end of that whining," says Torres with satisfaction. News of Morton's sudden departure spreads through the organization like wildfire. Foster drops in to Smith's office to express his relief. Fernandez also visits Smith and asks whether she is changing enough to keep up. "What do you think, Susan?" Smith asks. Fernandez replies: "Maybe I need to find the time to attend more Lean meetings in the workplace." "Sounds like a great idea," says Smith. "I also think I should have tried harder to influence Morton," Fernandez continues. "Whether that would have worked is something we'll never know," responds Smith. "Let's focus on the future. Susan, do you know where you want to go with the division, particularly in terms of the role Lean has to play?" Fernandez replies: "Patterson already asked me the same question. If I'm honest, I'm not really sure. I'm only just starting to realize how much effort I was putting into simply keeping things running." Smith offers to help come up with a vision together, while they wait to see who the new operations manager will be.

What a pain, Smith thinks to herself. Her next step is to call Jessica Kern and ask about formalizing staffing for the Lean team. Kern promises to drop in soon to discuss the matter. "We need to take a good look at how we handle that, because there isn't a specific budget right now," she says. "Fine, let's take a closer look at it next week," replies Smith. "Then we can also discuss further staffing for the Lean team; I'm almost done creating an initial outline. I know we still have a few months, but as far as I'm concerned, we should try to get everything in place so we can get off to a running start."

Change

That weekend, Smith continues working on her internship report. This rekindles her interest in change principles, and she decides to do a little more reading. She also dives into the master's thesis she got in Oregon. It's clear to her that she shouldn't try to dump Lean onto the organization and pray for the best. The relatively gradual, participatory approach she used in the ER seems to suit her better. When she discusses this with her husband, he says: "Don't underestimate the part you played, you provided a lot of support for the learning process. I think that's why you've gotten this far." "What do you think that means for the team I want to create?" asks Smith. "I think you need to focus on training your own people, rather than bringing too many outsiders. The latter could be viewed as an 'invasion' if you're not careful." "So you're saying I should look to recruit from within," says Smith, "although that means I'll be pulling a lot of good people away from their departments, which creates problems there. Some reorganization is fine, of course, but it's something to keep in mind. But getting back to change management," says Smith, "if I translate your interpretation to De Caluwé and Vermaak's color prints (see Box 5.4), we need to go for a 'green print,' an approach where learning experiences are key, right?" A few hours and a bottle of wine later, Smith and her husband go for an evening stroll to clear their heads. They agree that anchoring Lean requires blueprint elements in addition to a greenprint approach. Setting a clear course and not deviating from primary goals is an essential part of Lean.

On Monday, Smith meets with McLaughlin and her team leaders to discuss the true north for the ER. They quickly conclude helping the patient as quickly as possible is of primary interest. One of the team leaders recently made in inventory of average wait times, and the numbers are sobering. Patients have to wait for a good 40 minutes on average, and times of over an hour are not unusual. Smith thinks their true north should include a wait time of zero. McLaughlin is on board, but a number of the team leaders feel that's a bridge too far. They finally agree on striving for a true north with a wait time of no more than

15 minutes. Everyone leaves the meeting in high spirits after Smith emphasizes once again that they need to work toward this goal in small but consistent steps.

Later on, she also discusses the issue with Fernandez. She thinks the wait time to strive for should be zero. "After all, it's a distant point on the horizon," she says, "and it's best to set the bar high—that means we can always do better. But this is a great start!" It's clear to Smith: reducing wait times for patients will be the core of the true north for the ER.

Together with Torres, Smith organizes a number of lunchtime meetings to generate support for the Lean program—essentially already fulfilling her future role as Lean program manager. They use the sessions to collect input for the program and the vision on care, which can be translated to a vision for Lean and the true north for the whole of Careville. Smith and Torres agree to visit all of the division managers together. "But we also need to be in the workplace, Luis," says Smith, "otherwise it's all for nothing." He wholeheartedly agrees. "You know," says Torres, "that's really something you should do with Patterson. Talk about commitment form the top! I'm meeting with the Board tomorrow, let me see how far I get. I'm curious to see how the lady and gentlemen feel about it. But do we have a sufficiently strong basis to support the suggestion," Torres goes on. Smith replies: "I think that a few examples from the ER could be used to make people realize matters are more urgent than they may appear. That will help us build consensus, I think. I also think Patterson's going to be a great ambassador for our cause, the trip to Oregon really did the trick." "Great, could you work out the details?" Torres asks Smith.

Smith finishes her internship report that evening and sends it to Agnes Karlsson, with a request for critical assessment. She also asks her colleagues in Oregon a few specific questions about the change strategy they adopted. Karlsson calls her later that evening, and they spend a long time catching up. Karlsson says she would like to visit Careville once they're a little further along. "Of course, we'd love to have you," says Smith. Karlsson suggests that Smith ask Margo Davidson about change strategies: "she's got a strong theoretical grasp on the subject matter."

In the meantime, Smith has been asked to join the committee to select Cameron Morton's successor. The Lean leader profile she developed proves to be a key contribution to defining the job profile. The committee members quickly agree that the old profile for operations management is no longer adequate. After two committee meetings, the profile is finalized and submitted to the Board for review. A short time later, she hears that Patterson had to work hard to get it past the Board: both other Board of Directors members had serious reservations about getting the operations manager more closely involved in the workplace; "that's someone who needs to keep an eye on the figures using management dashboards," said one of the members. However, Patterson played his part as Lean ambassador and remained firm: "Of course figures are important, but Operations also needs to contribute to our people's learning capacity, and that can't be done from behind a desk!"

The Program Takes Shape

The program slowly starts to take form in the following weeks. Patterson appoints the steering committee—Cardiologist Peter Jacobs, care managers Susan Fernandez and Ellen Kowalski, and the future head of the ER: Jonathan Foster, who eagerly accepted the position after careful consideration. Patterson is willing to chair the committee himself, though he intimates he will have Torres represent him on occasion. In the meantime, Smith has managed to get both Linda Townsend and Robert Quinn on the Lean program full time as soon as it launches. For now, they are primarily focused on the ER, but they are already making inroads in a number of other departments.

Because a lot of the bottlenecks appear to affect late and night shifts, Smith decides to work nights for a few days. She hits pay dirt on the first night: a patient is admitted with severe heart failure, is stabilized in the ER, and it's clear he can't be sent home. The ER doctor calls Cardiology for a bed, to no avail. "We're fully booked, plus I'm understaffed," says the on-call nurse. The doctor doesn't give up easily, but she can't make any headway. She calls Internal Medicine, but there are not any beds there either. It would seem Surgery doesn't dare admit a cardiac patient. It takes exactly 35 minutes—Smith is keeping time— before they find a solution. A bed is finally found—just in time, following two more calls by the ER doctors—and the patient is admitted to Cardiology. "How often does this kind of thing happen?" Smith asks the doctor. "Ah," she replies, "at least once per shift." "What if you need another bed?" "The whole thing starts over again," she replies. It is quiet in the ER now, so they discuss the matter further. "According to me," says the doctor, "there are always beds available. Of course there are times a ward really can't handle a new patient, but I simply do not believe that's the case every night. Everyone is protecting their own little fiefdom, and nobody seems to want to help the ER. It's ridiculous, because it's supposed to be about the patient first. Bouncing the problem seems to be the norm," she concludes with a sigh. "Close attention and determination will be needed to get people to change here. And while we're on the subject," continues the doctor, "I also noticed patients regularly remain admitted for longer than medically indicated while I was an intern on the ward. There's room for improvement there too!"

BOX 6.1   THE IMPROVEMENT KATA

Box 5.2 about coaching leadership introduced a key tool for improvement, which Toyota has refined to an art form: the improvement kata. Mike Rother described this cyclical and consistent approach—which requires close attention—in great detail. This box presents a detailed overview of the improvement kata, using quotes and schematics by Rother (2009): the how, why, and what.

We pay close attention to this, because leader coaching and development skills belong to the essential "soft" success factors for Lean. All too often, leaders focus primarily on harder, quantitative success factors, such as the number of people trained, how many improvement weeks have been realized, and how many improvement activities have been completed.

Rother describes the essence of the kata in relation to the crucial role of the Lean leader as follows: A kata is a routine that is used to teach and affirm know-how. The (Japanese) suffix kata means "way of doing." A kata is a pattern of behavior, form, or routine that may be practiced until it becomes second nature (habit). This practice is focused on developing mindset and skills. This is how the kata forms a link between leadership, continuous improvement, and sustainability.

Katas may be considered educational and training routines for transmitting proven techniques. Within Lean, an essential leadership task is to have employees practice continuously and support them. A characteristic feature of Toyota's management approach is that the improvement kata is applied every day, by all employees. To understand the essence of the improvement kata, it is important to contrast it with traditional management beliefs and related tools. These are also focused on improvement, but are generally *product* oriented, while the improvement kata is explicitly and consistently *process* oriented (see Table 6.1).

(Continued)

BOX 6.1 (*CONTINUED*) THE IMPROVEMENT KATA

TABLE 6.1

Traditional Management versus Toyota Kata Management

Traditional Management Focus on Solutions	Toyota Kata Management Focus on Developing and Reaching Solutions
• Achieving goals • Looking for problems • Formulating solutions • Integrate stimuli • Do not interfere and check periodically	• Achieving goals • Strengthen problem-solving skills through practice and coaching … • … using a uniform procedure, such as the improvement kata

Repetition is a key characteristic of the improvement kata: continuous reflection, honing, and new attempts. There is no waiting until the next biannual performance review or biweekly meeting. The improvement cycle is an integral aspect of *daily* employee activities; the manager and employee maintain frequent and intensive contact.

The improvement kata focuses on short-term improvements that are consistent with the long-term vision and ambitions of Lean: true north. It is a systematic procedure that works toward ever improving performance in four steps. The improvement practice is key in a Lean organization:

1. Understand the course: what challenges are we trying to realize, what is our true north?
2. Understand the current situation: what are the current work patterns?
3. Define the target situation: what work pattern do we want to see in a few weeks?
4. Moving toward the target situation via plan–do–check–act (PDCA)—using the five questions: the step-by-step journey of discovery leading from where we are to where we want to be.

This also reveals the different roles managers and leaders have. The former is responsible for the improvement kata, the latter for vision and direction. The *development* of learning employees, not just solving the problem or bottleneck, is key. The goal is to draw conclusions while learning, with support from a coach. Conclusions that people draw on their own are far more convincing than those supplied by others. After all, in sports, training consists of both practice and reviewing competition performance. Training and implementation must occur in parallel, continuously; it's not about training first, doing later.

The ultimate goal is to create a flywheel effect, which continuously pulls leaders and employees out of their *comfort zone*, teaching them to focus on realizing long-term ambitions through short cyclical improvements. This is achieved by always focusing improvement activities on reaching the target situation. Repeated experimentation with the development and testing of solutions—and of hypotheses about how to achieve them—allows you to continuously examine and strengthen your own and your organization's learning process.

(Continued)

BOX 6.1 (*CONTINUED*)   THE IMPROVEMENT KATA

The discussion about current functioning and desired improvements is always based on five standard questions:

1. What is the target condition?
2. What is the current condition?
3. What obstacles do you think are preventing you from reaching the target condition? Which *single* condition will you address now?
4. What is your next step (PDCA)? What do you expect?
5. When can we expect to see what we have learned from this step?

These questions are focused on framing the next step with an eye to the far future (question 1), elaborating it and evaluating it (questions 2–5). The far future condition is the "true north," the target condition a step along the way that you need to be able to achieve within 3 weeks.

After a tiring week—she is not used to shift work anymore—Smith returns to her regular rhythm. She immediately makes an appointment with Fernandez about the bed issues during night shifts. Fernandez is aware of the problem but hadn't realized things were that bad. "I worked four night shifts," says Smith, "and there were problems finding beds for 16 of the 37 patients who needed to be admitted." Fernandez listens and asks for more information about the circumstances and responds with uncharacteristic firmness: "Jeanne, I'm glad you've brought this up. We should be ashamed of ourselves, we don't want this for our patients or ourselves! There's a care manager meeting scheduled for next week, and I'll make this the primary issue. We need to do something about this quickly! Oh, and isn't this an important issue to include in the true north for the ER?" "Yeah, good point," replies Smith, "it definitely belongs there!"

The First Steering Committee Meeting

Smith wrote a memo on the change strategy she wants to implement for the first steering committee meeting, with valuable input from Oregon. She addresses the transformation Careville needs to undergo and describes the programmatic strategy she wants to deploy, "according to Boonstra" (Boonstra, 2010). A greenprint approach to change also fits this strategy well, as described by De Caluwé and Vermaak (2006). This leads to an interesting discussion within the steering committee. Fernandez wonders whether a more planned approach would not be better. "So a 'blueprint', speaking in terms of De Caluwé and Vermaak," she says. Smith is surprised that Fernandez has been reading about change management. Jacobs seems absent, but suddenly says: "Can't we just get started? I mean, I understand it's all complex, but I'm ready to go, and so is my department!" "Now, Peter, you and I both know that our organization is not known for its flexibility," says Patterson. "I'm convinced we'll do better if we deploy a solid strategy for implementing Lean. Remember what happened at the Robert Kennedy Hospital? They 'just started', and that didn't go well for them at all!" Jacobs grumbles, but finally says: "Fine, I'll trust Jeanne. If she thinks this is how it needs to happen, let's do it." Kowalski adds: "What's all that color stuff about, though? I mean, it rings a bell, but I don't really know the details, if I'm honest." "Well, you should have prepared for the meeting," says Jacobs, annoyed, "or just kept quiet." Patterson intervenes before things get out of hand and says: "Jeanne will be happy to explain it to you after the meeting, Ellen." That takes care of that, although the burden's been shifted to Smith now.

Fernandez is not ready to let it go, though. "I still want to bring it up one last time," she says. "If we don't follow a strict plan, I foresee ending up with a directionless mess. Looking for solutions together is all well and good, but how on earth will we ever reach agreement?" Smith replies: "That's exactly where the steering committee comes in. We all agree on the program goals, and unless I'm mistaken, they're supported by the organization. That means we have to set a straight course toward the vision. However, I'm convinced change will be more sustainable if we don't attempt to dump Lean on the departments, but allow people to discover what Lean can mean for their work and for them on their own. It's essential that we provide them with the necessary learning experiences. That's the core of the improvement kata, and the pilot in the ER shows it works." Torres adds: "That's true, but we're taking a major step now, if I'm understanding the literature correctly, and a planned approach is also important. It's the same at Toyota." In the end, the conclusion of this constructive debate is that a "blue-green" approach is probably best. Smith is tasked with elaborating the plan.

At the end of the meeting, Smith's program plan is largely approved, including the budget; the only thing that needs adjustment is the change strategy. In addition, a date has been set for the official kickoff, in the presence of the entire steering committee. Smith will look for a location in the workplace, in the spirit of Lean. Patterson wishes Smith all the best and adds they will meet again soon in the workplace. Finally, he urges all steering committee members to frequently visit the workplace, attend Lean sessions and coach their employees. "If we lead by example, other managers can't help but follow," he says. Everything required for a successful launch of the Lean program seems to be in place. Smith can't wait to get started. At the same time, she's very motivated to make her final months in the ER a success and make sure Foster gets off to a good start.

In the weeks after the steering committee meetings, Patterson personally attends a number of Lean sessions. The topic of discussion is the wait time, which is now being recorded for each patient. Variability is large, but a pattern is starting to emerge: wait times are longest between 2:00 PM and 10:00 PM. The reasons for this appear to be diverse, from understaffing to slow patient transit. This quickly leads to frustration for a number of participants. "It feels like we're drowning in a swamp of causes, all of which seem to be valid," says one of them. Smith jumps in and explains that this is what Lean is all about: "Paying attention to the little things may make thing appear to move slowly, but if we work on it every day, we ultimately move forward. If we really only needed to deal with a few causes, we would have identified and resolved them a long time ago." Smith suggests drawing up a list of various causes and prioritizing them, starting by addressing the most common one. Fernandez and Patterson jump in when the issue of bed availability arises: "That's a hospital-wide issue, and we'll take care of that!" "Finally," one of the team leaders sighs with relief as she leaves the meeting with Smith.

Fernandez, who seems to be getting a feeling for this, participates in a session every week. She soon asks Smith how on earth she manages to cram all of the Lean activities in her agenda. "I really can't get anything done, Jeanne," she says in frustration. Smith knows the feeling: "The mistake I made in the beginning was thinking Lean just gets added on, and that nothing needs to make room for it. After weighing my options for a long time, I made two choices: I delegated a lot of my work, and decided I 'simply' wasn't going to do some things." "Like what?" asks Fernandez. "Mostly I cut back on reporting and so-called mandatory work meetings, and I also temporarily shelved a number of active projects." "That's pretty drastic," says Fernandez, "but did it help?" Smith replies: "It certainly did. I was convinced a major intervention was needed, and it really made a difference. Now I block the first hour and a half of my workday to spend in the workplace. I know that sounds like a lot, but I'm beginning to reap the benefits. Now that I'm closer to the workplace, I notice the problems when they're still small and easier to resolve than they would be if I only discovered them much later." Patterson also drops in on Smith. "How are you liking the Lean sessions, Bob?" she asks him. "Well," he replies, "they're very interesting, but it's not easy to figure out what role I should be playing, never mind making a contribution." Smith replies: "Maybe you could ask Ingrid Pearson how she does it, she's got years of experience after all."

A New Operations Manager

The job opening for an operations manager at Careville proves popular, and the number of applicants grows daily. Twenty candidates remain following initial selection by HR, and are submitted to the selection committee. Although most candidates have the right qualifications, only three really stand out to Smith. When she tries to determine what this choice is based on, she comes to the conclusion it is all about how the letters are written; some candidates explain how well they can lead and manage, others are proud of cost cutting or reorganization processes they have lead, and only a few write about how he or she has developed in recent years and is ready for a new learning experience. This learning experience links these three candidates to Lean, though none of the three have been involved with it directly. That is too bad, thinks Smith, but she had not come across much direct Lean knowledge or experience among the other candidates either.

Smith enters the meeting with the selection committee with her top three candidates in mind. Fernandez has a very different list, but Torres and Smith appear to be on the same page. Kern asks a few pointed questions: "Why did you choose these candidates, specifically?" Smith justifies her choice, explaining the "will to learn" was the deciding factor for her. Torres adds: "Of course we need somebody who can manage the division, but considering the Lean transformation we're involved in, we can't risk having someone there who doesn't understand or doesn't want to understand Lean, and acts accordingly." After some consideration, Fernandez agrees: "I hadn't looked at it from that angle, but you're right." Four candidates are selected and invited for an initial interview.

In the meantime, Smith is busy looking for a few Lean consultants. She finds to staff consultants within the organization who have followed a Lean course and would like to grow into full Lean consultants at Careville. Smith carefully breaches the matter of their change in position with their managers to avoid any issues. She also attracts a few external consultants, including one of Foster's former colleagues, who brings along a few years of experience.

Then it is time for the interviews with the candidates for the operations manager position. The first candidate is relaxed and calm, and speaks with enthusiasm about a major organizational change he just completed in his current position. "What would you do differently if you had to do it all over again?" Torres asks him. The moment he responds with "nothing, actually," Smith writes him off as a serious contender. "What key points you learned from this process would you take to Careville?" Fernandez asks next. "Taking time to do things," he replies almost instantly. "What else?" Smith follows up. "Um, putting the right people in the lead," he responds, somewhat less confident. "And what kind of people would those be?" Smith continues. "Well, your followers, the smart kids," he responds.

The interview with the second candidate is extremely pleasant. He is humble and asks pointed questions about the introduction of Lean at Careville. When they ask him what he has learned from the change processes he was closely involved with, he replies: "I've learned to listen carefully to what is being said, but particularly to what is not being said. Based on that, I had a lot of individual discussions with people, always asking about the reasons for their reservations about the changes. That revealed a lot of the insecurity was based on ignorance. But they often did have a useful answer to my question about how they could conquer that ignorance. We could usually find a way to answer their questions together." "That took a lot time, I assume," Fernandez asks. "That's true," the candidate replied, "but it only cost me a couple of months spread across the entire project, and the result is broad support for the changes made." Smith is impressed by this candidate.

The third interview takes a different turn. The woman they talk to knows a lot about change management, so the discussion quickly shifts in that direction. She listens to Smith explain the Lean program at Careville, and says: "Interesting, I think that would require a "blue-green" approach—to use De Caluwé and Vermaak's terminology—maybe with a 'whiteprint' coating." Torres and Smith exchange looks, and Torres says: "Good to hear you draw that conclusion, it's exactly where we ended up." In order to allow comparison with the other candidates, Kern asks this one for her most important learning experiences from change processes. The candidate replies: "I think a mix of coaching of those involved and giving them the opportunity to learn a lot is key. That took some getting used to in an organization that had always been run by the numbers, but doing things that way also taught me and the organization a lot."

Candidate number four withdrew his application at the last minute, leaving the committee to evaluate the three interviews. The selection committee quickly agrees: the first candidate would not be invited back, but the other two will be. Patterson and Fernandez conduct the two follow-up interviews together with the division director with support from Kern. During the second interview, they ask the candidates to work on a case study, and the way they approach it is the deciding factor. They choose Marjorie **Walker**, despite the fact that Fernandez would prefer not to see another woman in her division's management structure. Walker formulated an elegant, believable approach to the case study. Her elaboration also showed leadership, without ignoring the necessary management and administration aspects. She asked a number of relevant questions: What was patient satisfaction at Careville? How many safety incidents do you have here? Do you have data on average wait times at the outpatient clinic? In short, she made it clear she not only put the patient first, but also acted on it. Finally, the extent to which Walker emphasized the importance of using the right language when introducing Lean was noteworthy. That was a real eye-opener for the committee members.

Fortunately, employment terms were quickly agreed upon, and Walker can get started right away (see Box 6.2).

BOX 6.2   LEAN AND LANGUAGE

Care institutions—like all organizations in a variety of sectors—have their own jargon, acronym culture, and ritual language use. This is generally extremely functional. After all, a daily exercise in creative language use would quickly become tiresome. It could also lead to misunderstandings. At the same time, major transformations such as Lean demand attention for language use.

(Continued)

BOX 6.2 (*CONTINUED*)   LEAN AND LANGUAGE

Why Is Language So Important for Transformation?

Each major change is associated with the risk that (senior) employees are left with an impression it is all the same meat, different gravy. "Well, we did that three reorganizations ago, and back then we called it xyz. Just keep your head down, it'll pass." Continued use of everyday language strengthens this feeling. Transformation requires original, innovative language; language that expresses urgency, ambition, and motion.

So Should Everything Be Renamed?

That's the other extreme. Excessive use of new language can lead to estrangement or even rejection. Particularly if the innovation is rich with its own (odd) terminology, as is the case with Lean. People should not be left with the impression Japanese is the new company language. At the same time, consistent use of explicitly Lean terminology— within reason—*can create a sense of unity.* If done well, it can almost become a talisman.
  This means:

- First, use standard language to announce the transformation.
- Introduce new terminology clearly and gently, preferably accompanied by a clear translation.
- Continue to pay attention to the introduction of new language, within reason, while respecting existing terminology.
- Approach old language use with reason. Employees do not need to be reprimanded if they refer to a "spot on the horizon" instead of the true north. Give them the opportunity to make the new terms their own; the message and meaning is sometimes more important than precise choice of words.

Is It Only about Jargon?

It is also important to pay attention to positive, activating, and motivational language use:

- Try to speak and write about Lean in positive terms; all too often, we spend too much time describing what something is *not*, while stating what it *is* often makes a far more powerful statement (so: try to avoid denials).
- Describe what employees can expect, and what is expected of them in concrete terms. Avoid vagueness, assumptions, and words that express delay.
- List the advantages and expected yields not only on an organizational level but also in terms of departmental and individual interests. People want to know what they stand to gain.
- Use concrete examples to clarify abstract ambitions and developments. Colleagues can be used as ambassador for this. Employees prefer to hear good news from each other than from a relative stranger.

(Continued)

> ## BOX 6.2 (*CONTINUED*)   LEAN AND LANGUAGE
>
> ### *In Closing*
>
> Because language use and presentation are such sensitive topics, we recommend always following the four eyes principle: if you put something on paper or want to present it, always have at least one other person check your design, preferably some-one not closely involved in the matter. Demand critical reflection from this person:
>
> - Are you showing enough respect for company culture?
> - Are your statements formulated originally and innovatively enough?
> - Are you translating enough, actively building bridges between the old and the new?
>
> Walker shows Smith that she may not have given enough attention to communi-cation and language. For example, she may not have invested enough in building bridges between the old and the new in her dealings with Fernandez and Morton; in transitioning from their own familiar terminology and mindset to the newness of Lean. She may have been trying to move too quickly.

Beyond the ER

Fernandez is true to her word, and discusses the bed issue in the care manager meeting. She drops in on Smith to talk about how things went. "Actually," says Fernandez, "there wasn't much to discuss, because everyone immediately agreed we need to help every patient. But I did figure out why it's turned into such a problem a lot of the time." "Do tell," says Smith, "I'm all ears." "Well, Surgery has a long waiting list that they're trying to clear, and they like to keep beds free for that—which I can understand. And Cardiology has a budget problem right now that they're working hard to address, and an extra admission during the night does nothing to help matters." "I get that, but the patient is the one paying the price," replies Smith. "That's true," says Fernandez, "but we also noticed something else. Overnight hospital admissions without a medical indication are more common than you think. For example, because the fam-ily doesn't have time to pick someone up. And the doctors don't put up much of a fight in those situations." "And what did you conclude?" asks Smith. Fernandez responds: "We agreed that each of us would indicate within a week what the bottleneck is per ward, and will present that to the Board of Directors. The doctors will also need to make new agreements about discharg-ing patients." "Good, I'll discuss that with Carl tomorrow," replies Smith. "Let's be honest, though. We know we have an average of 35 admissions per day, there's got to be some way to plan for that. Are we making a mountain out of a molehill here?" "Yes, I completely agree, but my colleagues aren't quite there yet," Fernandez sighs in frustration.

It is taken a while, and the appointment has already been changed three times, but Smith finally sits down for a meeting with Cardiologist Peter Jacobs. He starts with a very practical issue: "You know what bugs me? You use a different form for the patient chart in the ER than we do, so it always takes us a while to figure out what you actually did down there." Smith resists the urge to address the content of the comment, and replies: "That's a great example. Value stream mapping will immediately highlight that. The solution may end up being sim-ple." "What do you mean, 'may'?" asks Jacobs, slightly irritated. "Look," replies Smith, "you and I both immediately agree that the fact that we do this differently isn't handy. But we use a single standard form for all patients, regardless of their presenting complaint." "And we use the form we've agreed to state-wide, making it easier to transfer patients to other hospitals if necessary," responds Jacobs. "This isn't an issue we should try to resolve here and now," says Smith in response, "but it's certainly one we need to address." They agree the first step will be to check whether both forms are really necessary, and also look at how big the differences really are. They will examine potential solutions once that is clarified.

Together with Fernandez and McLaughlin, Smith finally defines the true north for the ER. Negligible wait times and "a bed for every patient" is the core. The latter means that a bed is immediately available in the right ward for every patient they stabilize in the ER. "I like this approach," says Fernandez. "We'll need to overcome quite a few challenges before we're even close to achieving these goals, but we've taken the first steps. Mark my words, the whole bed issue is far from resolved, considering some of the issues I've heard about. And the employees seem to be letting circumstances get to them and don't have the energy to think about possibilities." In the meantime, McLaughlin has agreed to discuss the problem with his fellow department heads.

On Marjorie Walker's first day, Fernandez takes her on an extensive introductory tour, beginning with a stand-up meeting in the ER. Walker is impressed and asks a few pointed questions, making a good first impression. Walker and Smith have an in-depth discussion later that week. Smith tells her about the Cardiologist, Jacobs, who did an about-face once he witnessed what Lean could do for his specialty firsthand in Oregon. "Now he's a real pioneer here," says Smith, "and he's dragging a lot of other specialists along in his wake. It's really something."

Reflection

After an educational experience in Oregon, Smith is back at Careville UMC. She is in charge of the ER again, and spends more time in the workplace, even working a few night shifts. We see how valuable that turns out to be, and how serious a bottleneck that is invisible "during the day" can be. The bed problem during the night shift makes the importance of good communication between various departments abundantly clear. Management has a key role to play, as the groundwork for good cooperation (also) needs to be laid at the top. Fernandez shows she understands this, and takes the initiative to address the bottleneck in the appropriate forum. It also becomes clear the problem does not only lie with the care managers: doctors also play a role in the availability of beds. This underlines the importance of a strong "guiding coalition," which can ensure necessary steps are quickly taken at the right level. Depending on the outcomes of that meeting, the Board of Directors may need to weigh in, for example, "every bed at Careville is for the patient." So if a specialty needs to borrow a bed, there is no room for discussion.

In addition to regular job performance, we also see Smith lead by example. By meeting the challenge head-on and solving problems in a disciplined way, she also works on developing her own problem-solving skills. She learns to translate the sometimes odd and abstract Lean concepts she picked up in Oregon into practical behavior that anyone can see and copy. She needs to learn to think and respond differently, particularly during a crisis.

It is very important for Smith and her team to define a vision in the form of a true north, and set direct course toward it. By doing so, they put their reputation on the line, and clearly define the direction of the desired improvements.

Additionally, we see as Smith tries to make the most of the available momentum by already taking steps toward the future Lean program management and her role in it. This will allow for a smooth start when the time comes.

Lean Leadership Attributes

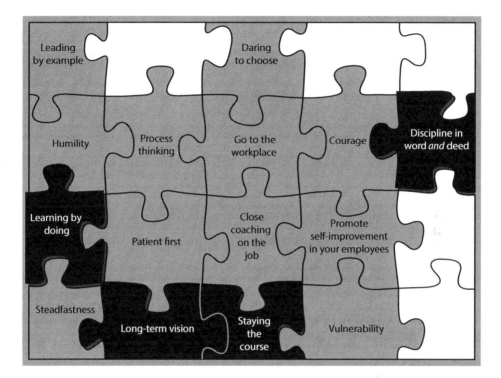

7

Lean Leadership

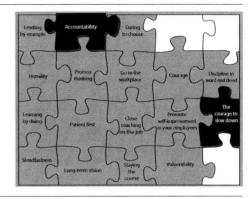

Case Study

The Lean program is actually launched a good 6 months after Smith's return from Oregon. During that period, Smith has personally seen how important interdepartmental cooperation is; initiating the necessary attitude shift is going to be one of the major challenges. Smith's transfer to the Lean program also means Jonathan Foster's appointment as head of the emergency room (ER).

Lean Program Kickoff

Smith walks into the hospital on Monday morning and starts heading to the ER before remembering she has a new office now. Old habits die hard. The new office is furnished, but still quite bare. Quinn and Townsend drop in shortly after that, with an equally uneasy look on their faces. After sharing a cup of coffee, they discuss their plan for the first week and get to work.

Later that week, on a rainy Thursday afternoon, the Lean program is officially launched. Not in the boardroom or some fancy hall, but in the workplace on the Cardiology department. And in keeping with Lean, it's not Smith or Patterson who launches the project, but an ER team leader. She briefly talks about how her work has changed over the past year, thanks to Lean, and recommends everyone at Careville to take part. "Witnessing how we identify small problems and come up with long-term solutions on a daily basis is really great," she says enthusiastically. "And long-term means these bottlenecks are gone for good." Next, a few people from her team present some concrete examples: reduction of wait times and incidents, more efficient workplace organization, improvement in supply management and organization of the treatment rooms and other workplaces, and much more. The assembled crowd has all kinds of questions, so many that Smith intervenes. "It's great you have so many questions," she says, "We'll drop in and address them in greater detail later, but I suggest we move on to the next subject." Townsend presents an outline of the Lean program and the approach it will take. "In short," she says, "we can't handle all of the departments at the same time, and we've decided to focus primarily on those who cooperate closely with ER first. We'll slowly expand from there." Cardiologist Peter Jacobs closes the meeting, enthusiastically sharing what he saw in Oregon: "I never realized there was so much to improve in Cardiology, but it's really possible, I witnessed it personally!" (See Box 7.1)

BOX 7.1   PROGRAM MANAGEMENT

A (pilot) project management approach was selected for introducing Lean in the ER. This was a good fit for the nature and scope of the results desired at that moment. Expansion and further implementation of Lean in other parts of the organization are quickly placed on the agenda, making it necessary to formulate ambitions at the organizational level. That is a good time to switch to a program-based approach. This box examines program management and its differences with project management in more detail.

A program is a unique and temporary sum of projects and activities that must be performed in a controlled and coherent manner. These efforts are focused on achieving one or more complex (strategic) goals. Management is focused on achieving goals and managing risks. Steering is too complex for the normal operating procedures within the organization. The differences between programs and projects relate to quantity, timelines, and scope. Many subprojects do not necessarily make a program; that requires more. While a project focuses on achieving a predefined *result*, a program is focused on striving toward different, sometimes difficult to reconcile *goals*. This means program management happens at a higher strategic and more coherent level than project management. Thus, a program requires a different structure and different management tools.

In short, although there are parallels to be drawn between programs and projects, which may make it appear a program is merely a bigger version of a project, it is worth spending time examining the differences. These differences are presented in Table 7.1.

Like a project, a program has elements that allow course adjustments. However, these are distinct in each case and operate at a different aggregate level. Program management often uses the TFEFG management tools, which stand for tempo, feasibility, efficiency, flexibility, and goal orientation. Project management usually utilizes TOMIQS or a variation thereupon. This acronym stands for time, organization, money, information, quality, and scope.

TABLE 7.1

Differences between Programs and Projects

Object Aspect	Program	Project
Timeframe	Temporary, stops as soon as possible and necessary	Finite, margins predefined
Focused on	Predefined goals	Predefined result
Decision making	At fixed times, based on program plans	Based on decision documents per phase
Plan of action (process)	Planned in coherent sections	Phased in logical steps
Outcome	Unique, coherent, dynamic, desired	Unique, one-off, complex, desired
Institution actors with respect to cooperation	We want to work toward it together	We need to build it together
Management	Using tempo, feasibility, efficiency, flexibility, and goal orientation	Using time, organization, money, information, quality, and scope

The Lean program kickoff was very well received, and the number of departments that are contacting Jeanne Smith's Lean team on their own accord are growing. It takes some careful diplomacy to explain that they cannot start everywhere at the same time. Smith is happy that her team is being expanded, because she is already shorthanded.

The Lean Team Is Complete

The next week, five new Lean consultants start work in the Careville Lean program. Smith's team is now at full capacity and she organizes a team day so people can get to know each other and to work on a joint approach. "Because I want us to present a unified image, show people we have a shared approach," says Smith. "Of course everyone is free to adjust the details, but our approach should appear uniform." As Townsend and Quinn were responsible for setting the "Lean tone" at Careville, their approach is used as a starting point. Once they have presented it, the discussion begins. During an intensive afternoon session, the approach is discussed in detail and honed on a number of points. Smith is a bit worried that Quinn and Townsend are being taken on too hard, but when she checks with them during a short break, she finds the opposite is true. "This is great, Jeanne," says Townsend, "the essence of our approach is still in place, and we've already made a few good improvements. For example, we're combining coaching and an improvement culture, but remembering we also need to show short-term results. Those things are complementary, because quick, visible results are crucial for change!" "It's all very Lean," grins Quinn. "And a good example of the green and blue change strategy," adds Smith. After a hard afternoon of work, it is time to relax over dinner.

That weekend, Smith and her husband take the boat out, but there is hardly any wind to be found. As they sit there, waves gently lapping at the hull, her husband asks: "Have you talked to your colleagues in Oregon recently?" "Actually, now you mention it, it's been a while," says Smith, "I simply haven't found the time with everything that's been going on. And I never heard back from Jacob, he was going to respond to the Lean leader profile." As there is no sign of the wind picking up, they head back into port—with the engine—and are back home early. "Tom, I'm going to send a quick e-mail to Agnes, just to check how things are going," says Smith. Karlsson replies on Monday morning, saying she is very busy, but that she would like to make a Skype appointment with Smith to get an update on how things are going at Careville.

That Friday afternoon, Smith and Karlsson catch up. It is a busy time at the Robert Kennedy Hospital (RKH), mostly because they are busy merging with a nearby regional hospital. "And Jeanne, they don't do anything with Lean over there," sighs Karlsson. "We get to start all over again." The merger also explains why Jacob Vargas never got back to her: he's got his hands full with the HR implications of the merger. "So your plan to move Lean to the next level is still sitting in a drawer," says Karlsson, "but it is at the top of the pile, you can be sure of that. As soon as the dust settles, we'll get right on it. And we'll also drop by to visit you guys," Karlsson promises again. "That would be fantastic," says Smith, "because we're starting to gain some momentum, and I'd be interested to hear your feedback." "What did you guys settle on as your true north?" asks Karlsson. "We defined three pillars," replies Smith: "First: patient satisfaction of at least 9/10, second: no avoidable medical errors and third: wait times of no more than 5 minutes for patients." "Wow, that's ambitious!" says Karlsson. "That's true, but we expect it will take years to even come close to reaching those figures."

Then Smith asks: "What about your Lean team, that's been in place for about a year now, right?" "Yes, that's right," says Karlsson, "and without the merger, I thought we would be able to dissolve it in another year or two, but I think that'll take a little longer." "What's the next step after you dissolve the Lean team?" asks Smith. "My goal is to make a number of managers responsible for 'maintaining' Lean knowledge within the organization and safeguarding the philosophy." That's music to Smith's ears. "What about new managers coming in without Lean knowledge and experience?" "Then it's up to the current staff to train them," says Karlsson, "so we need to make room for that."

"How did things go with that weirdo, Morton?" Karlsson asks next. "Oh, didn't you know? He left us less than a week after our visit to you," says Smith. "His replacement started a few weeks back." "So did you manage to find a more modern leader?" Karlsson asks. Smith describes Marjorie Walker, and says working with her is really inspiring. They chat for a little while longer, and it is already late by the time Smith goes to catch her train. While she is waiting for it, she runs into Torres and tells him about her discussion with Karlsson. "It can't be a coincidence," Torres replies, "Patterson already asked me when she was coming here."

Discussions with the Pharmacy

Smith has held another meeting with the head of the pharmacy, Frank Johnson, hoping to involve him in the Lean program. And although the worst of the chill is gone, there is not a great deal happening yet. Smith cannot put her finger on where the resistance is coming from. She goes to Torres for advice, who tells her the pharmacy has been under pressure for a long time. "Personally, I think Frank's not a good fit in the team, which means the entire pharmacy is underperforming. The Board has tried to do something about it, but without success until now. I think it is best you first try division management," concludes Torres.

Smith decides not to wait, and immediately makes an appointment. The talk with division management provides some information—they feel the pharmacy is doing "fine," but that so many costs have been cut and there is nothing left to gain. "That's why we understand that they can't really go along with your plan, Jeanne," says the care manager. Smith says that she tried to explain how Lean will also lead to improvements in the pharmacy, but that the message still has not sunk in. Division management agrees they will raise the issue. At the end of the meeting, Smith says: "I really hope we can find a solution, because we managed to do some great things with the lab.* So much went wrong between the ER and the lab that one in every thirty tests had to be repeated. That was not just the lab's fault; we made number of improvements in the ER as well. And yes, the team leaders and I really had to stay on top of things to make sure the new routines stuck. There are still a few employees who fall back on old habits, so we need to remain vigilant."

The meeting about the pharmacy with division management yields results quickly; Johnson drops in with Smith "to explain a few things." He explains that division management has been breathing down his neck for a long time, because a lot of mistakes were made in the past. "Despite the fact that we're performing above average now, I felt like I'm still on probation," sighs Johnson. "I'm worried starting with Lean means something I have no control over, and if I make another mistake, that's it for me!" "I understand your dilemma," replies Smith, "but Lean is all about getting rid of mistakes!" "Yes, you've explained that to me before, but how do I know we won't create more problems before we fix some?" asks Johnson. "Why don't you visit the lab?" says Smith, "we had some fantastic results there." Johnson finally agrees, and they both attend a stand-up meeting in the lab the next morning.

After the meeting, they talk to the head of the laboratory, who tries to encourage Johnson: "I know you're under a lot of pressure, Frank," says Al Assaf, "but the same is true for me. Now that we're introducing Lean here, all of the problems are getting smaller, it's great! It took us a good deal of effort to provide the results faster, but now the doctors have them when they need them. First of all, that's much better for the patient, but I've also noticed

---

* The lab is part of the same division as the pharmacy.

the doctors really value the service—some of them even drop in personally to say so! The benefits are also significant for my own people. They get a lot fewer annoyed people calling and asking about results." Johnson says he had no idea Lean had these kinds of results. "But now that I've seen how it can work, I want to get right on it," he says enthusiastically.

It takes another week, but then it happens: Johnson contacts Smith with a request to join the Lean program. Smith has to restrain her happiness. Instead, she says she is very pleased with his decision and is willing to make room for him. Johnson apologizes for his resistance—he is not too proud to admit when he's wrong. They shake on it, and make an appointment to launch Lean in the pharmacy. Smith decides to give the job to Townsend, she thinks that will be a good fit for the pharmacy team. She also drops in on Torres to share the good news. "Well, it was about time," he grumbles, but Smith can see that he's just as pleased as she is. "So the visit to the lab did the trick?" he asks. "I think so," says Smith, "when Frank saw what was happening with his own eyes, he caved."

Leadership

Foster invites Smith for a brief meeting. Because Smith misses talking to him, she proposes they take a little more time to catch up properly. Although Foster's very busy, he agrees. After a brief chat, Foster says: "The main reason I asked for this meeting is that we've got major problems with beds during the night shift. Things were better for a while, after Fernandez made some agreements, but the problem is back with a vengeance now," he says. "I personally worked a few night shifts to keep track. The doctor needed more than half an hour to handle over half of the requests, and more than 45 minutes in 20% of cases." "That's pretty bad," says Smith. "Do you have any idea why the agreements Fernandez and Patterson made six months ago aren't working anymore?" "I'm not exactly sure, but I have noticed people are falling back on old patterns. It seems like it's all about the beds, rather than the patients," says Foster. "I also discussed the matter with McLaughlin and Fernandez, and they couldn't put a finger on it either." "That's all good and well, but it is their responsibility," says Smith. "They need to show their worth and tackle the problem head-on. Come on, we'll go see Fernandez right away." Unfortunately, Fernandez is out of office, and her schedule is booked solid for the rest of the day according to her secretary.

"What about the boards displaying available beds?" asks Smith. "They're still being used, but not as consistently as they were. We don't always get a call, and we sometimes need to check ourselves, or we find out the numbers are wrong," says Foster.

A few days later, Foster and Smith talk to Fernandez. She listens to what they have to say, and responds: "Right, so we're reverting back to old habits. I get it, it's time for me to get on top of things. Which of the departments present the biggest bottlenecks, Jonathan?" "It's the usual offenders—Cardiology and Surgery," replies Foster. Fernandez immediately picks up the phone and calls her colleague over at Cardiology. She tells Fernandez that she has not given the matter any attention, and is sorry to hear things are back to the old situation. "But I really don't have time to do anything about it right now," she adds. Fernandez is not satisfied with the answer: "Sorry, but we have a clear, simple agreement that we both believe in, so I'm counting on your cooperation." After a bit more discussion, Fernandez's colleague promises to get things done within the week. The next call is to Ellen Kowalski, who is responsible for the surgery department. "Is that really true?" asks Kowalski after hearing what is going on. "I'll get right on it. We made very clear agreements about this with the departments." "Did you discuss this with McLaughlin yet?" asks Fernandez. Foster says he has. "He almost blew up, and immediately went to Surgery to deal with the issue," says Foster.

"Well, let's keep a close eye on this," Fernandez says to Smith and Foster. "And make sure you contact me if you notice another relapse like this, we really need to avoid that. We are already involved in the ER," says Fernandez, "but how are things going there, Jonathan?" "Pretty good," says Foster, "but I've noticed the tendency to fall back on old habits is tough to break." "How do you deal with that?" Smith asks him. Foster explains he mostly tries to coach his team leaders to make sure they keep their teams sharp. "And if we notice a relapse, we address it immediately during the next stand-up meeting," he concludes. Just as Smith and Foster are about to leave, the phone rings. It is Ellen Kowalski, who tells her she discussed the bed issue with one of the night shift team leaders. "There's more to it than I thought," says Kowalski, "the hiring freeze that was announced recently means we have major staffing problems. I'm going to need some more time to crack that one. I'm still committed to the agreements we made, though."

Within a few days, Foster is asked to attend a meeting with the team leader and the resident by the head of Surgery. Smith joins as an observer. Everyone quickly agrees about the target situation, where the number of available beds needs to be provided at the end of each day shift. "What's stopping you from doing it?" asks Smith. "We just haven't been focused on that over the past few weeks," replies the team leader, "in part because the doctors' handoff also moved to a different time. So we need to pick a fixed time where you, the resident and I come together," says the department head. "And we need to make it a permanent scheduled item. I'll make a proposal," says the head of Surgery. The resident adds that they have also discussed the fact that patients sometimes remain admitted for longer than medically indicated. "We're pretty strict now," she says, "a patient can only stay past the planned discharge date if the treating physician provides permission. And the department head keeps close tabs on things." Smith and Foster leave the meeting satisfied. "Sometimes it's the simple things that are difficult to hold on to," they conclude. In any case, the first step has been taken.

A Visit from Oregon

The delegation from Oregon is here for a working visit to Careville. Karlsson flies in a few days early, to give her and Smith the chance to lay the groundwork for the exchange. It's great meeting again, and the days fly by. Karlsson provides extensive feedback on what she observes and the Lean team hangs on her every word. "But make no mistake," says Karlsson: "I'm learning a lot from this as well, and I've seen a few things I can apply back home. For example, you're ahead of us when it comes to making the agreed upon changes visible and ensuring the agreements are kept. We can learn from that! Falling back on old habits is a problem we face too, and I don't feel like we've got a firm grip on it. Your improvement boards are also much better located than ours, there's no avoiding them. I'll be discussing how we can implement that as quickly as possible next week. The last thing I'd like to mention is the system of shift handoffs at the bedside, which allows the patient to ask any questions immediately, that's something I want to introduce as well. I noticed that clears up a lot of misunderstandings!"

The rest of the party arrives on Wednesday evening: Davidson, Vargas, and, of course, Pearson. Thursday is all work, and they exchange impressions late that afternoon. "You've come a long way in a short time," says Karlsson, "I'm really impressed. I'm particularly impressed by your persistence in sticking to the stepped expansion plan. We succumbed to pressure from other departments who wanted to join in earlier than planned far too often, which led to a number of problems. We usually weren't able to deliver due purely to capacity issues." Davidson compliments the Careville crew on their choice for Morton's replacement. "I'd hire that lady in a heartbeat," she tells Torres. "It's great to see how Marjorie is pulling her division forward." Vargas adds that he would like to talk to the HR department at Careville about the Lean leader profile. When it's time for dinner, Patterson and Pearson excuse themselves: "We've got something to discuss, so we won't be joining you."

On Friday, the full delegation discusses the true north statements of both hospitals. The differences aren't huge, they quickly conclude. Next, they look at the effect of Lean on "the management." Kowalski and Fernandez explain how their work has changed with the introduction of Lean. "Heading out into the workplace and participating in Lean sessions was a little scary in the beginning," says Fernandez, "but now that I'm used to it, I can really see the benefits. Always viewing the primary process from the patient's perspective is absolutely crucial. I get the feeling we can really make a difference. It's also very tiring, because it takes a lot of time!" "Sounds familiar!" laughs Davidson. "What did you do to keep things manageable?" she asks Fernandez. "Well, I took Jeanne's advice and scrapped a few 'regular' projects to make more time for both myself and the teams. That gave us a lot of breathing room. Another one of Jeanne's tips was to get rid of or cut down on a lot of the "traditional" meetings. The stand-up meetings greatly reduce the need for weekly meetings." Karlsson responds: "It's a good idea to scrap current projects early. Looking back, we did the same thing in a more passive way; a few projects simply died a quiet death from neglect." "You do need to consider that prematurely stopping projects won't make you any friends," says Kowalski. "Susan and I cut about eight projects in total, and that created a heck of a mess. But we're still behind the choice we made back then," she concludes.

The discussion continues. Smith indicates that she feels management still needs to remain involved with the change activities. The Oregonians agree. "For a while, we thought the departments could handle it on their own," says Karlsson, "but in the end, the departments are too focused on their own needs, and not on the patient." "It's understandable," adds Davidson, "after all, results are the only thing that used to count. We're trying to shift that mindset and emphasize that every employee is jointly responsible for the total results of our hospital." Fernandez agrees: "If I don't continuously emphasize the interests of the patient, I've noticed attention flags. But I also need to work hard to get colleagues at my own level from other divisions involved—for example, with the issue with the beds during night shifts. I have no problem with the occasional sales pitch for Lean, seduction is part of the game!" (See Box 7.2)

BOX 7.2   SEDUCTION IN BUSINESS

The introduction and application of Lean is so extensive and intrusive that it requires a broad array of tactics to present Lean in a positive light. After all, attention to content alone is not enough in this day and age. Everyone needs to support their message, to pay attention to packaging, and thus to the messenger. This is something also felt by charities, civil society, and religious organizations. Celebrities are frequently used to "seduce" target groups.

The introduction of Lean is impossible without mastering the art of seduction. Due to the professional context, we do refer to this as "seduction in business." Lean leaders who understand this art are an asset because their valuable message

(Continued)

BOX 7.2 (*CONTINUED*) SEDUCTION IN BUSINESS

and promise for the future can then reach a broad and receptive audience. The Careville UMC case study shows how differently people can respond to the new developments Lean entails. Smith has it hard with her division management: Morton takes the cake when it comes to negativity, but Fernandez also isn't quick to commit to Lean.

The suggestions in this box regularly address the issue of "dealing with resistance"; see also Boxes 2.1 and 2.3.

THE PROFESSIONAL CONTEXT IS DIFFERENT ... AND YET THE SAME

To get colleagues on board with major transformations like Lean does not require the building of lasting romantic relationships or friendships. That would be inappropriate and confusing. However, it is useful to view a number of issues that apply to personal relationships within a professional context. Such as friendliness, alacrity, being open to others, true attention, and careful listening. These are examples of basic principles that apply in personal life and that are—oddly—occasionally forgotten in professional life.

THE CARROT OR THE STICK?

A well-prepared, positive, enthusiastically presented message, with coherent verbal and nonverbal communication, is more likely to succeed than a dog-and-pony show. A smile, lively intonation, supporting gestures, positive terminology (what will happen rather than what will not), a creative setting, or framework. These are all methods for supporting your story and showing your own belief in it. Those less talented in this domain would do well to learn, practice, and ask for support.

During a walk around the ER, Smith tries to "sell" Lean to Morton and Fernandez with a smile and enthusiasm. This helps support Fernandez's increasing interest in the effects of Lean.

THERE IS NO INTEREST LIKE SELF-INTEREST

We often tend to mention advantages and gains of major changes in general terms and at an organizational level. We often forget that most people wonder: "What's in it for me?" The art of seduction in business lies in translating the positive message to the "public" and tailoring it to departments, teams, positions, or even individuals as required.

PRESENTING THE UNPRESENTABLE?

Only extremely charismatic, practiced speakers are capable of convincing large groups of people directly and collectively, although the question of how sustainable this conviction is remains (e.g., consider politicians). A person who wishes to radiate belief and positivity need not reach for hyperbole, as this is more likely to raise suspicion than gain trust. A strong story with properly supported claims flourishes better in a realistic framework than in an overly optimistic one.

(Continued)

> ## BOX 7.2 (*CONTINUED*)   SEDUCTION IN BUSINESS
>
> This also applies to disadvantages and bottlenecks. Trying to justify everything or downplay problems may provide temporary comfort, but may leave listeners feeling like they have been told a fairy tale. Disbelief and resistance will come up later, with interest. You are more likely to seduce your audience into buying into your story if you are honest about bottlenecks and downsides, and present them yourself.
>
> ### ONE BY ONE
> We see Jeanne Smith struggle with a number of her colleagues, her manager of operations Morton, most of all. For a long time, she chose to resist these people in public. Though brave, this is rarely effective. It is better to address the matter head-on and take people like Morton aside for a face-to-face discussion. This is no guarantee for success, but does show the other that things are serious, that you want to commit. Seduction in business is being open to the other, listening, asking the tough questions and taking the time to do so. It also requires a personalized approach, tailored to address the objections and worries of the other. It often means more than one meeting is required; time and perseverance are essential.
>
> A good way to involve opponents is giving them an active role. A person who has to work with a new concept himself will be quicker to see advantages than one who only hears of it. Smith applies this principle by repeatedly asking Fernandez to attend a stand-up meeting—and her persistence pays off. It is worth noting Smith could support her arguments by pointing out the negative consequences of not attending stand-up meetings to Fernandez.

Next, Jacob Vargas outlines how he introduced Lean in the Human Resources (HR) department. "First off, it was tough going," he confesses. "There was a lot of resistance from both team leaders and employees." "Why is that?" asks Smith. "Good question," replies Vargas. "I think the biggest problem was that most people thought we didn't have a problem." Torres asks: "So how did you deal with that?" "Well, I asked a few managers how long they had to wait for a recommendation if they had an issue with an employee," says Vargas. "The average time was about three weeks, while such questions are often urgent. When I confronted my department with the issue, it slowly started to get through. That was the opening I needed to start introducing Lean, slow and steady, and the average 'delivery time' for a recommendation has been reduced to twelve work days. There's still room for improvement, but it's a start."

Next, Margo Davidson talks about how well Lean was perceived by the public back in Oregon. "We held an open house to show people how our methods had changed awhile back. Each department opened its doors to patient organizations, medical journalists and other interested parties, with the intention to let them experience the benefits patients have reaped from something as seemingly abstract as Lean. It was really great to see our people proudly present the fruits of their labors. I'm sure that open house was the reason for a number of very positive stories about RKH in the media, and that's something we still benefit from," concludes Davison. Smith thinks to herself that they should do something similar in a year or so.

The final subject of the meeting between the two parties is "the Lean leader." Both sides have thought long and hard about an ideal profile for someone like that. That evening, Smith writes a summary of what they discussed. You can read more about the Lean leader profile in Box 7.3.

BOX 7.3   PROFILE OF A LEAN LEADER

Hundreds of books have been written on leadership. The differences between leaders are enormous, and the similarities often too general to allow significant conclusions to be drawn. Leadership cannot be captured in a formula, after all. We can work to increase our understanding thereof and provide meaning within certain contexts. That is what we have attempted to do by creating a Lean leadership profile. This is a thought experiment, a characterization. There is no such thing as the one true road to leadership—that is a road that must be explored together.

A leader is a person who inspires people around him to embark on a journey toward a challenge destination. In addition, a Lean leader is also capable of clearly formulating a vision of the future and taking his (or her) people along in developing and shaping this promising vision. Creating value for the patient (or client, in other organizations) is the key. It requires the courage to challenge the status quo day in, day out. The Lean leader links this to the discipline required to work toward the set goal in a structured, consistent manner. His statements and actions represent the behavior required for a successful company.

A Lean leader may be recognized by the people around him; they are continuously developing and also capable of identifying problems that prevent the organization from reaching the desired goal on a daily basis and resolving them sustainably. A Lean leader trusts his employees, and dares not only to give responsibility to people in the workplace, but also sees it as his duty to coach them and increase their capacity for solving problems. This coaching involves an active presence in the workplace, where the coachee works. He recognizes that he does not have all the answers, and helps the employee analyze the situation, formulate solutions, and test these solutions in daily practice.

A Lean leader has a clear image of a future goal, extreme focus, and a strong sense of direction. He also allows for maximum flexibility. A Lean leader trusts in the ideas and cooperation of the entire team and gives employees a strong voice in the decision-making process. The Lean leader must be able to facilitate and support, must be humble, and recognize his limitations. He must also be responsible for others and set goals for them, be visible, ensure that employees are valued at their worth, and above all, display the courage needed to change the status quo. Each and every day.

A Lean leader is not afraid to experiment and test hypotheses by visiting the workplace himself. Lean leaders are familiar with fundamental procedures and have a good feel for identifying what is truly important. They can simplify complex problems by working together with the team to find the best solution. Lean leaders do not manage numbers, but processes. The yield of the process, not the financial result is of primary importance. They do not immediately present

(Continued)

BOX 7.3 (*CONTINUED*) PROFILE OF A LEAN LEADER

solutions or draw conclusions, but try to understand the situation, always asking: why? "No problem is the only real problem!" Lean leaders are not only good teachers: they are primarily coaches, capable of creating an organization that learns continuously.

Lean leaders focus on ever-improving results and therefore regularly participate in value stream mapping, stand-up meetings, and improvement initiatives themselves. A Lean leader is completely dedicated to a life of learning, is curious and persistent. To him, failure means insufficient understanding of the root cause, and thus an opportunity to try again and again. A Lean leader considers problems to be personal challenges, which provide the potential to add new or more value to patients, employees and the organization. A Lean leader never stops communicating and enjoys asking others questions and supporting them in their development. He is completely congruent and disciplined in his behavior. He sees every deviation from leadership as waste. He is humble, knows he is not smarter than anyone else, and still has a great deal to learn. He knows how to lead and serve at the same time, he is consistent and yet flexible, a generalist and yet an expert, combines willpower and humility, and follows the rules yet knows when to make an exception. Is the Lean leader a needle in a haystack? Or is he a master at combining these contradictions? How this is given form will become clear as the puzzle we have created along the way takes shape.

Reflection

The Lean program at Careville UMC is off to a strong start, thanks to solid foundations laid in the ER. It is clear that Lean is mostly something that takes place in the workplace, but intensive involvement from management is required to address a number of bottlenecks. It also needs to be emphasized continuously that the interests of the patient are of primary importance. This demands a cultural shift that cannot be realized overnight. RKH is a perfect example—they have been working based on Lean for a few years, but putting the patient's interests first still needs emphasizing. Therefore it is important that management also think and work in a Lean way.

Lean leaders must be the very picture of discipline and responsibility. They must meet the expectations they have of others. They must hold themselves accountable, just as they required others to hold each other accountable. People follow the leader—make sure you send them in the right direction.

And finally, to truly succeed with Lean requires guts, because it means making major changes to operations and maybe even initiate major remodeling. For example, the nursing ward in the RKH, where a major remodel was required to improve logistics.

How this is given form is reflected by the puzzle we have created along the way and present below.

We have left a number of pieces open on purpose. Lean means continuous development and improvement, and this also applies to the leader. Because every situation demands different emphasis, we do not pretend this puzzle is ever complete. We do think it provides a clear image of the properties we believe a Lean leader should possess. We hope this will serve as an aid and inspiration for your own daily practice.

Lean Leadership Attributes

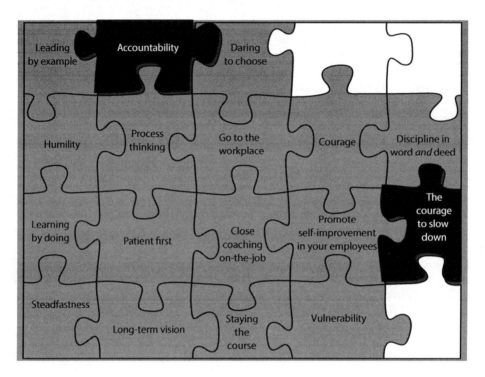

8

Years Later

Case Study

Years have passed. Careville UMC has developed into a Lean hospital with an international reputation. Careville's production numbers have increased significantly and patient satisfaction is the best in the country for the second-year running. The number of medical incidents has dropped so low that the health inspection has asked questions about it. Under the watchful eye of Jeanne Smith, the Lean team has reached all of Careville's departments. And now, with the program's goal achieved, it's time to end it (see Box 7.1 on Program Management).

The Last Steering Committee Meeting

In close cooperation with Luis Torres and her faithful second in command Linda Townsend, Smith has drafted a memorandum for the Lean steering committee. In this memo, she presents the successful achievement of the Lean program's goals. That means 100% of Careville UMC—all of the departments and all other units—are operating according to Lean philosophy. There are also enough managers at various levels who have mastered Lean well enough to introduce newcomers to its arts. Torres already announced the planned end of the Lean program—with Marjorie Walker, who took over from Bob Patterson. Patterson has retired, and the word is he has moved to Oregon.

Walker opens the meeting and welcomes everyone. "This is a special meeting," she begins. "If everyone agrees, it's time we dissolve ourselves." They discuss Smith's memo; there are not many questions. Ellen Kowalski asks about the "true north" they defined at the start of the program. "We haven't gotten there yet, after all," she says. "That's right," replies Smith, "and it remains to be seen whether we ever will; it's a goal on the horizon to strive for, to continue working towards. There will always be room for improvement. But looking at the numbers, we're well on our way: patient satisfaction is now a good 8/10, up from 7/10, wait times have been more than halved, and the number of medical errors has been reduced enormously." "That's true," says Walker, "but continuous budget cuts mean there are new challenges to be faced. I'm afraid we'll have to maintain this high level with even less budget. Lean is no magic wand, but I'm confident we need not fear any challenges now that we've mastered this philosophy. We've also garnered a lot of goodwill with many of our stakeholders, which benefits us compared to other hospitals. So no, we're not done, but things are looking fantastic!"

Fernandez has something to add: "I've had preliminary access to an ongoing study into 'best employers,' and Careville is head and shoulders above the rest of the statewide competition," she says. "That's mostly due to two factors: mutual respect and trust between employees, and the ample room for growth we provide for everyone. The upside is that this makes us very popular in the job market. While other institutions are having major difficulties attracting new staff, we've got the cream of the crop knocking at our door. That makes achieving our improvement goals a lot easier."

The steering committee decides it is time to end the program and dissolve the committee. Smith is asked to organize a fitting closing ceremony, with internal and external parts. "I think we need to thank everyone here," says Walker, "but also show the outside world exactly what we've achieved."

After the meeting, Foster says to Smith: "The timing may seem odd, but I need to tell you something. I accepted a new job as Lean program manager at a general hospital in the city yesterday. I hate to leave, but this is a golden opportunity for me." Smith gives him a hug, and tells him he is right to go for it: "Congratulations, Jonathan! Someone with your skills should always be looking for new challenges. It's a loss for Careville, but turnover is good for us. And since you're not moving too far, we can still meet for drinks from time to time," she adds. "What about you, Jeanne?" Foster asks. "Well," she says, "it's not official yet, so hush-hush, but I'm probably going to fill Ellen Kowalski's position. She's due for retirement soon."

The Festive Conclusion of the Lean Program

Smith has organized a fantastic event to celebrate the end of the Lean program. The day is filled with workshops that take place in the workplace. That took some organizing, because normal operations needed to continue. Creative scheduling and limiting group size made it possible, however. Of course, participants are expected to make a contribution to improve the value streams at Careville.

The festive part of the day for employees begins at half past three. The time was selected to allow both day and evening shifts to participate in the festivities. An enormous Japanese buffet has been laid out in the restaurant, which has been decorated to match. The catering department got a number of useful tips and hints from Robert Quinn, who recently went on his dream trip to Japan. He traveled the land of the rising sun for 6 weeks and—of course—toured a number of Toyota factories.

When most attendees have arrived, Walker takes to the stand. "First of all, I shouldn't be the one standing here—one of you should be. Lean belongs to all of us, and we all work hard to make it a success. But because today is a turning point in the way Lean is anchored at our hospital, I would like to take the opportunity to share a few things with you." She hands the microphone to Susan Fernandez next. Fernandez outlines in clear, concise terms how she was pretty skeptical about Lean at the beginning, and how a visit to the workplace with Morton and Smith marked a turning point for her. Walker closes: "We didn't come here to give speeches, but to celebrate how far we've come together. But there are some people we do need to thank: the Lean team has done a fantastic job, particularly their leader, Jeanne Smith!" Once the applause has finally died down, Walker says:

"To end on a positive note, I have two more announcements. First, I will take ownership of Lean in the coming years. Because I think making sure Lean is firmly anchored at the highest level of the organization is essential. Second, I'm extremely pleased to announce that Jeanne Smith has been nominated to replace Ellen Kowalski, who will be going into well-deserved retirement tomorrow."

After the speech, Smith is congratulated by many of her colleagues. After congratulating her, the head of the operating room tells her that Cameron Morton is back in town. "He's working as Lean coordinator for a construction company now, isn't that something!" A while later, during a quiet moment, Smith sends Agnes Karlsson a quick message to tell her about the great party. Karlsson replies immediately, "What are you going to do now?" Smith sends back a quick message, promising to call Karlsson the next day. The phone call turns into a long Skype session, ending with an agreement to go sailing on Puget Sound soon.

Epilogue

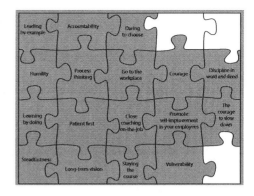

We apply Lean management within our organization on a daily basis and face the challenges this presents day in, day out. The manager's role is always the key. We notice schedules are overflowing and understand how difficult it is to formulate a clear vision and work toward achieving it. This requires the ability to see past the horizon and the perseverance to maintain a steady course in that direction. At the same time, we also demand a coaching attitude, an eye for detail from a manager, for example, if he or she is observing the process of distributing medication on the ward.

These contradictory properties are not always easy to unite in a single individual, which is what makes Lean so challenging in daily practice. Does the ideal Lean leader exist, and if so, what does he look like? This question inspired us to write this book.

Jeanne Smith took you along on her journey of discovering what Lean means. The resistance and problems she faced are typical of what we see in daily practice. She started by hiring two Lean advisors, but quickly discovered you cannot delegate Lean, and shifted her attention closer to the workplace. This revealed problems that are often not captured by standard management reports, but do affect the primary process. Addressing them and making sure they end up in the right place is difficult if "the system" is not designed for this. In Oregon, she saw exactly what Lean can do and what it demands from hospital management. True Lean leadership was present there. This inspired her to take bigger steps toward Lean leadership and a Lean organization together with others from her own hospital.

This does not mean Smith's journey of discovery is finished by the end of this book. Lean means continuous development and improvement, and this particularly applies to the leader. We are also not saying the puzzle is complete. We hope we have given you a solid foundation for defining the profile of the ideal Lean leader and translating this to your own daily practice. Writing this book was an inspiring process for us. We look forward to discussing the insights in this book with you, and lifting them to the next level. We hope our book will benefit your Lean journey and enhance the great potential it has for our organizations.

Kjeld H. Aij and Bas Lohman

Lean Leadership Attributes

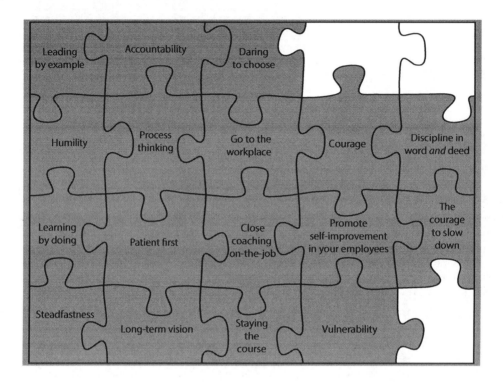

References

Benders, J., M. Rouppe van der Voort, and B. Berden (eds.) (2010). *Lean denken en doen in de zorg. Acht verhalen uit de praktijk*. The Hague, the Netherlands: Boom Lemma uitgevers.

Benders, J. and M. van Bijsterveld (2000). Leaning on Lean. The reception of a management fashion in Germany. *New Technology, Work End Employment*, 15(1), 50–64.

Bennis, W. and B. Nanus (1990). *Why Leaders Can't Lead* (pp. 16–22). San Francisco: Jossey-Bass Publishers.

Bennis, W.G., K.D. Benne, and R. Chin (1979). *Strategieën voor verandering*. Deventer, the Netherlands: Van Loghum Slaterus.

Bennis, W.G., K.D. Benne, and R. Chin (1985). *The Planning of Change*. New York: Holt, Rinehart and Winston.

Boonstra, J.J. (1992). Developing fundamental organizational change. *Research Notes from the Netherlands*, 4(2), 8–11.

Boonstra, J.J. (2000). Leren veranderen. *M&O, tijdschrift voor Management en Organisatie*, 54(1), 81–86.

Boonstra, J.J. (2010). *Leiders in cultuurverandering. Hoe Nederlandse organisaties succesvol hun cultuur veranderen*. Assen, the Netherlands: Van Gorcum.

Collins, J. (2010). *Good to Great. Waarom sommige bedrijven een sprong maken… en andere niet*. Amsterdam, the Netherlands: Business Contact.

Covey, S., A.R. Merrill, and R.R. Merrill (1994). *First Things First: To Live, to Love, to Learn, to Leave a Legacy*. New York: Simon and Schuster.

De Caluwé, L. and H. Vermaak (2006). *Leren veranderen: een handboek voor de veranderkundige*. Deventer, the Netherlands: Kluwer.

Drucker, P.F. (1957). *Management in de praktijk*. Bussum, the Netherlands: G.J.A. Ruys Uitgeversmaatschappij.

Goleman, D. (2012). *Over leiderschap. De beste leiders gebruiken hun emotionele intelligentie*. Amsterdam, the Netherlands: Business Contact.

Katzenbach, J., I. Steffen, and C. Kronley (2012). Cultural change that sticks. *Harvard Business Review*, 90(7/8), 10–17.

Kets de Vries, M. (2007). *Leiderschap ontraadseld*. The Hague, the Netherlands: Academic Service.

Kotter, J.P. (1996). *Leading Change*. Cambridge, MA: Harvard Business Review Press.

Kotter, J.P. (1997). *Leiderschap bij verandering*. The Hague, the Netherlands: Academic Service.

Kotter, J.P. (1999). *What Leaders Really Do*. Boston, MA: Harvard Business Review Books.

Krafcik, J.F. (1988). Triumph of the Lean production system. *Sloan Management Review*, 30(1), 42–51.

Liker, J.K. (2004). *The Toyota Way: 14 Principles from the World's Greatest Manufacturer*. New York: Free Press.

Liker, J.K. and D. Meier (2006). *The Toyota Way Fieldbook*. New York: McGraw-Hill.

Liker, J.K. and G.L. Convis (2012). *The Toyota Way to Lean Leadership. Achieving and Sustaining Excellence Through Leadership Development*. New York: McGraw-Hill.

Maxwell, J. (1998). *The 21 Irrefutable Laws of Leadership*. Nashville, TN: Thomas Neville Publishers.

Mintzberg, H. (1973). *The Nature of Managerial Work*. New York: Harper-Row.

Mintzberg, H., B. Ahlstrand, and J. Lampel (1998). *Strategy Safari. A Guided Tour Through the Wilds of Strategic Management*. London: Prentice Hall.

Pfeffer, J. and R. Sutton (1999). *The Knowing-Doing Gap: How Smart Companies Turn Knowledge into Action*. Cambridge, MA: Harvard Business School Press.

Rother, M. (2009). *Toyota Kata. Managing People for Improvement, Adaptiveness and Superior Results*. New York: McGraw-Hill.

Rouppe van der Voort, M. and J. Benders (eds.) (2012). *Lean in de zorg. De praktijk van continu verbeteren*. The Hague, the Netherlands: Boom Lemma uitgevers.

Spear, S.J. (2004). Learning to lead at Toyota. *Harvard Business Review*, May 2004, 78–86.

Spears, L.C. (2004). Practicing servant-leadership. *Leader to Leader*, 34 (Fall 2004), 7–11. www.greenleaf.org.

Ten Have, S., W.D. Ten Have, A.B. Huijsmans, and N. Van der Eng (2015). *Change Competence: Implementing Effective Change*. New York: Routledge.

Van Geloven, M., P. Fest, and T. de Roos (2012). *P² Care. Project and Portfolio Management in Health Care*. The Hague, the Netherlands: Boom Lemma uitgevers.

Weggeman, M.C.D.P. (2007). *Leidinggeven aan professionals? Niet doen!*, Schiedam, the Netherlands: Scriptum, p. 259.

Womack, J.R. and D.T. Jones (2003). *Lean Thinking: Banish Waste and Create Wealth in Your Corporation*. New York: Free Press.

Womack, J.R., D.T. Jones, and D. Roos (1991). *The Machine That Changed the World*. New York: Harper Perennial.

Index